Making a Difference

Making a Difference: Careers in Health Informatics
addresses everyday questions from people interested in
working in health informatics. Typically, this includes people
who work in health care, computer and technology fields,
information science, finance / insurance and related areas. The
book aims to tell students about various jobs that exist in the
health informatics field, what credentials they need to qualify
for those jobs, and a brief description about what people in
those roles tend to do every day. As faculty members teaching
in a Master of Science in Health Informatics program, we
are fortunate to have eager, bright, and talented graduate
students who are invested in related health informatics areas.
This could be their experiences in medicine, nursing, clinical
care, software engineering, finance, business, library science,
data science, or caregiving. Common questions we hear from
our students that may be similar to questions among readers
include: 'what jobs are out there?', 'what can I do with this
degree?' or 'what does a health informatics specialist do?'
If you are asking these questions or it is your job to answer
these questions, then, yes, this book is for you! **Too often
people feel stuck.** It is important to look up and realize you
can add value in different ways in this expanding field. As you
read this book, we want for you to realize that you have
options. It is our aspiration that this book helps you on your
journey, providing a path forward.

The book examines career options, roles, and skill sets
important in health informatics across 6 related industries.
We want readers to realize that their skills and interests can
apply in many areas of the field, not exclusively hospitals.
This book highlights 6 unique work segments (hospital

systems, long term care, health IT / consumer health organizations, government, consulting, and payer / insurance companies) into which readers may look to expand their career opportunities. The hope is that this book will provide insight into career opportunities students and professionals may be qualified for, and interested in, but of which they are simply not aware. Hiring managers and human resource professionals across stakeholder groups may also find the book helpful in learning about other roles that may benefit their organizations.

Making a Difference
Careers in Health Informatics

Rebecca Meehan and John Sharp

Routledge
Taylor & Francis Group

A PRODUCTIVITY PRESS BOOK

First published 2024
by Routledge
605 Third Avenue, New York, NY 10158

and by Routledge
4 Park Square, Milton Park, Abingdon, Oxon, OX14 4RN

Routledge is an imprint of the Taylor & Francis Group, an informa business

ISBN: 978-1-032-02903-0 (hbk)
ISBN: 978-1-032-02902-3 (pbk)
ISBN: 978-1-003-18572-7 (ebk)

DOI: 10.4324/9781003185727

Typeset in Garamond
by Apex CoVantage, LLC

Dedicated to our students and those who see the value of technology, data and information in improving health and healthcare.

Contents

10 Career Phases and Next Steps 169

Acknowledgments

This book would not have been possible without the help of many of our colleagues in the field of health informatics. Throughout the book, you will see quotes and experiences from several of them, including:

- Edward Marx, CEO of Divurgent and author of *Healthcare Digital Transformation*
- Tim Sobol, MS, PMP, BRMP, Senior Program Manager, UC Davis Health
- Mandi Bishop Meyers, Healthcare Industry Analyst, Gartner
- Lygeia Ricciardi, Founder, AdaRose
- Mark Dill, Principal Consultant, tw-Security
- Jon Mertz, Founder, Sante Fe Innovates
- Dr. Jason Gilder, Informatics Scientific Subject Matter Expert federal contractor supporting HHS ASPR BARDA Division of Research Innovation and Ventures (DRIVe)
- Dr. Shauna Overgaard, Mayo Clinic
- Devendra Rao, Executive Director & Business Partner, Information Technology at Blue Cross Blue Shield Association
- Lorren Pettit, CEO GeroTrend Research & VP Digital Health Analytics, CHIME

- John Derr, Founder of LTPAC/Health IT Collaborative, Chief Clinical Technology Advisor
- Sandy Hebert, Director of Product Analytics, PointClickCare
- Marcia Conrad-Miller, Digital Transformation Leader & Consultant, former VP of Consulting Services, CGI
- Tyler Allchin, Managing Director, Healthcare at JobsOhio
- Jessica Pollock, Senior IM Business Analyst, Midwest health insurance company
- Dawn Dumm
- Peter Kress, Senior Vice President and Chief Information Officer of Acts Retirement Life Communities
- Dr. Majd Alwan, Chief Strategy and Growth Officer, ThriveWell Tech
- William Vaughan, former Chief Nurse, Office of Health Care Quality, State of Maryland

Also, we acknowledge the invaluable review and comments from Jessica Pollack.

We appreciate the assistance for editing and research from Allison Madar and Dr. Yue Ming.

With true appreciation of the discussion, review and unending support from our families and our spouses, David Adkins and Janet Sharp.

Finally, we would like to recognize the Health Informatics program of the School of Information at Kent State University (www.kent.edu/ischool/health-informatics) and the talented students whose questions about career opportunities were the impetus for this book.

About the Authors

Rebecca Meehan, Ph.D. is Associate Professor in the School of Information, Health Informatics program at Kent State University in Kent, Ohio. Dr. Meehan earned a doctorate in Medical Sociology and Gerontology at Case Western Reserve University in Cleveland, Ohio. After working in applied research to improve quality of life for patients in hospital and long-term care settings, she took a role as a senior user experience researcher and later a product manager for a global enterprise level software group. Dr. Meehan brings her experience in software development and applied research to her academic role at Kent State. With a focus on health informatics education, her research involves improving the user experience of health information technology, across the care continuum, to improve patient safety and decrease clinician burden. Dr. Meehan has authored many journal articles and served as a reviewer for several peer-reviewed journals. She has presented at national and global conferences as an educator, advocate and researcher in health informatics.

 **John Sharp, MSSA, FHIMSS** has been Adjunct Faculty in the Health Informatics program at Kent State University since 2013, teaching clinical analytics. Previously, he worked for HIMSS and Cleveland Clinic. He has authored many journal articles and book chapters on health informatics, digital health, social media and chronic kidney disease. He has presented at several conferences in the U.S., Canada and Europe. He has advised several startups and is currently on the board of Reach Health. He serves on the editorial boards of Telehealth and Medicine Today and ICT and Health and is a reviewer for the *Journal of Medical Internet Research*. In addition, he is a fellow of HIMSS.

Chapter 1

Introduction

1.1 Who Is This Book for?

Students and professionals looking to make a career change have approached us as faculty members in a master's program in health informatics, conveying that they have heard that health informatics is a growing professional field where they can help people and make a difference in healthcare by working with data and information. Many students often convey that they need a change. They can be unsure about what options exist because their current experience is in one aspect of health care or a related field. They are looking for professional options that may not include working at bedside or directly with patients.

They ask questions including:

- What kind of job can I get in this area?
- How can I make a career change into this field?
- What if I've never worked in healthcare before?
- What if I have always been a clinician? Will I be able to make a career change into this field?
- What can I expect to do every day in this job?
- Do I need special credentials to get these jobs?

DOI: 10.4324/9781003185727-1

If you are asking these questions or it is your job to answer these questions, then, yes, this book is for you! **Too often people feel stuck**. It is important to look up and realize you can add value in different ways in this expanding field. As you read this book, we want for you to realize that you have options. It is our aspiration that this book helps you on your journey, providing a path forward.

In this first chapter, we will review:

1) What health informatics is, including the sub-specialties
2) The job outlook
3) Leveraging the experience you bring
4) The six health informatics work settings or ecosystems we focus on throughout this book
5) Elements of the changing work structures and how to access them

Let's get started!

Health informatics and health information technology constitute one of the fastest-growing fields for job opportunities. The demand for informatics professionals in healthcare continues to expand. This growth has been fueled over the past decade and a half by the rapid expansion and implementation of Electronic Health Records (EHRs), beginning in 2009 with the financial incentives from the Health Information Technology for Economic and Clinical Health Act (HITECH). Growth continued to accelerate with the rapid adoption of telehealth and related health innovations during the Covid-19 pandemic. In this short time, health informatics-related jobs have grown exponentially, as they are aligned with the data and information technology landscape. However, when professionals or students want to work in the field of health informatics, they often encounter no clear path or description of the kinds of work they'd be doing, what skills they may need, whether they are qualified or where these job opportunities exist. **The goal of this book is to shed light on career pathways and opportunities for those wanting to work in the field of health informatics.**

You may be a recent graduate or a student in health informatics or a related field. Perhaps you are already working in healthcare or are working in an entirely different profession outside of healthcare, but you are interested in making a career change. This book is for you! Those who began their careers in patient care may find a career shift to informatics an opportunity to fulfill their interest in how technology can better serve the clinical space. Those with a technical, business, financial, insurance, regulatory or social services background but have never worked in healthcare may see new projects in this growing field of health IT as a chance to use their knowledge and apply their skills to make a difference in new areas and to innovate. Because of the many job roles within health informatics, this book intends to present a broad landscape of the scope of the field and requirements. For those new to the field or still completing a degree, internships should be viewed strategically to obtain prime experience for a first job in informatics.

We will also address how to move into the field of health informatics and making further career moves once in the field. Discussion of career moves will include the importance of advanced degrees and certifications as well as continuing education. Project-specific experience, such as technology implementation or enhancement, can be the key to a promotion or lateral move to a more desirable position. Knowledge of healthcare functions in all of their complexities, as well as awareness of medical terminology, are a strong basis for a move into or within health informatics. For example, if you have been a part of helping a clinical unit convert from one electronic health record system to another, you would have garnered a wealth of experience in this multi-faceted project, working with a number of cross-functional team members; this would be applicable to another similar project of converting systems. Perhaps you were part of the group who conducted a workflow analysis for the organization or the unit, to help inform what the software should be addressing, in what order, and what related outcomes or artifacts should be a part of the process; this is also applicable to other health IT evaluations where a workflow is necessary to understand how the team functions, or how it should function. Or perhaps you are new to a clinical setting, but you have been managing a database in a financial field; these same database skills are applicable in healthcare.

1.2 What Is Health Informatics?

Health informatics is not one thing. Health informatics is multi-disciplinary and occurs at the intersection of 1) health and healthcare, 2) information technology and 3) social and behavioral science (see Figure 1.1). The American Medical Informatics Association (AMIA) defines health informatics as the science of how to use data, information and knowledge to improve human health and the delivery of health care services (AMIA, 2023). Job opportunities exist across a number of areas.

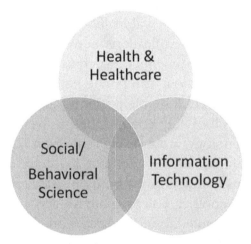

Figure 1.1   Health Informatics: Intersection of Multi-Disciplinary Fields.

1) **Health and healthcare** can be viewed from the perspective of clinicians, patients, healthcare systems, pharmacists, payers, researchers, health IT specialists, governments and care settings. Health informatics professionals help to inform and facilitate healthcare for all stakeholders along the care continuum, from communication between patients and clinicians for routine maintenance of health, prevention and wellness, to maintaining prescriptions at the pharmacy, acute care, outpatient, emergency department or urgent care visits, to short-term rehabilitation, home healthcare and long-term post-acute care. Complex health information needs to be accurate, timely and accessible to support decision making and inform the best care. Health informatics professionals from across disciplines work to make this possible.

2) **Information technology** is the study or use of systems for how health information is captured, stored and accessed. Technological advances in health information technology (e.g., electronic health records, medical imaging and scanning) and personal connected health (e.g., telehealth systems, health apps on our smartphones or wearable digital glucose monitors) make it easier to capture and monitor pertinent health and wellness information. In the United States and many countries globally, the most comprehensive clinical health information is captured, stored and analyzed by clinicians in the electronic medical record (EMR) of their medical office or hospital system. Patients can also access health information via a personal health record (PHR) or EMR portal.

Information technology advances in artificial intelligence (AI), machine learning, virtual and augmented reality (VR and AR) are transforming possibilities and experiences in healthcare. Not only are they becoming more numerous, but they are getting smarter, with better, more intuitive user experience, so that health information technology can be used across disciplines by clinicians, patients, researchers and administrators. Information and data science focus areas are essential for a strategic approach for data informed decisions. For example, health informatics specialists work with medical classifications, terminologies, knowledge organization and knowledge management to help store, link and access information to support analysis and communication in healthcare.

3) **Social and behavioral science** involves decisions individuals and families make about their healthcare, patterns of use by clinicians and clinical care teams and the extent to which all stakeholders use health information. For example, the cultural traditions of communities and individuals profoundly influence health information seeking, use of medical care and overall health behavior. Moreover, policies and practices instituted by organizations contribute to health informatics through the influence of the cost and payment structure of healthcare, privacy laws, infrastructure around technological ability and strategy to share health information.

We can begin to examine the major practice areas of the discipline.

- Consumer health informatics: Evaluating how patients and caregivers access and use health information
- Clinical health informatics: Evaluating health outcomes of individuals
- Public health informatics: Evaluating the health of groups of people or populations

The practice areas of health informatics can be considered part of information science, computer science, data science, business and analytics. Work opportunities and tasks within health informatics typically fall within these areas.

1.3 Informatics Specialty Areas in Healthcare

As we discuss career opportunities in health informatics, it is important to consider and define the many informatics specialty areas in healthcare, and know how they are related to each other (see Table 1.1). "Informatics" is a word used frequently across disciplines, and is defined as the science of

Table 1.1   Specialty Areas of Health Informatics

Discipline	*Definition*
Biomedical Informatics	Biomedical informatics (BMI) is an interdisciplinary field that emerged to improve human health by examining effective uses of biomedical data, information, and knowledge for scientific inquiry, problem solving and decision making (Faiola and Holden 2017; Kulikowski et al. 2012). Bioinformatics and health informatics are branches of BMI that examine data across the spectrum of human life, utilizing different research approaches, from basic research in bioinformatics protocols to more applied methods in areas of health informatics. ***Example of what you might do in this field:*** *Utilizing data mining and integration of disparate data sources to analyze genome sequences and how these affect human health.*
Medical Informatics	Medical informatics is central to BMI, and resides where computer science/information technology and medical care intersect. ***Example of what you might do in this field:*** *Refining a natural language processing (NLP) tool to analyze clinical and biomedical narratives from patient chart notes.*

(Continued)

Table 1.1 Specialty Areas of Health Informatics (Continued)

Discipline	Definition
Bioinformatics	Bioinformatics focuses on the micro components of human life and is the specialty area of BMI, examining the molecular and cellular level of basic research in health. Bioinformatics improves methods of storing and accessing biological data, as well as applies tools of computation and analysis to the capture and interpretation of biological data (Bayat, 2002). *Example of what you might do in this field:* *Modeling and displaying information using large data sets from cellular and genomic data.*
Health Informatics	Health informatics is "the interdisciplinary study of the design, development, adoption and application of IT-based innovations in healthcare services delivery, management and planning." (HIMSS, 2023). Health informatics includes three sub-categories: 1. consumer health informatics 2. public health informatics 3. clinical informatics *Example of what you might do in this field:* *Analyzing data for social determinants of health to inform a plan for community and population health improvements and interventions.*
Consumer Health Informatics	Consumer health informatics focuses on the patient's or the consumer's experience of how to access and use health information technology to improve health. This incorporates digital health tools including electronic health (eHealth) and mobile health (mHealth) applications (AMIA 2023). *Example of what you might do in this field:* *Conducting a user study of how patients utilize a phone app to upload their blood sugar levels to manage diabetes.*

Discipline	Definition
Public Health Informatics	Public health informatics applies computer science, technology and information to the study of populations of people and the practice of public health including surveillance, prevention, preparedness and health promotion (AMIA 2023). *Example of what you might do in this field:* *Transferring Covid-19 results gathered at hospitals and clinics through computer systems to federal, state and local health agencies for tracking and analysis.*
Clinical Informatics	Clinical informatics focuses on applied research in health information for individual patients. This is a field typically found across different settings, including hospitals, acute and non-acute healthcare settings, payers, research and consulting groups with a focus on improving clinical care (AMIA 2023). *Example of what you might do in this field:* *Helping to integrate diagnostic imaging into the EHR for improved patient health outcomes and reduce duplicate testing.*
Nursing Informatics	Nursing informatics is the specialty that integrates nursing science with multiple information and analytical sciences to identify, define, manage and communicate data, information, knowledge and wisdom in nursing practice (ANA 2014). The field also promotes user-friendly and patient-centric innovation to improve patient outcomes and enhanced clinical workflows by integrating the clinical and technical languages of health (HIMSS 2021). (https://www.himss.org/resources/what-nursing-informatics) Accessed May 30, 2023. *Example of what you might do in this field:* *Examine patterns of nurses' use of barcode technology during medication dispensing and administration.*

(Continued)

Table 1.1 Specialty Areas of Health Informatics (Continued)

Discipline	Definition
Pharmacy Informatics	Pharmacy informatics is the "scientific field that focuses on medication-related data and knowledge within the continuum of healthcare systems – including its acquisition, storage, analysis, use and dissemination – in the delivery of optimal medication-related patient care and health outcomes" (Blash 2021). **Example of what you might do in this field:** *Refine programming of alert alarms on smart pumps for patients receiving high-risk medications.*
Health Information Management (HIM)	Health information management (HIM) is the practice of acquiring, analyzing and protecting digital and traditional medical information vital to providing quality patient care (AHIMA 2022). It is a combination of business, science and information technology. HIM professionals protect the integrity of health information. Careers in this area utilize specialized certifications from a Certified Coding Associate (CCA) to a Registered Health Information Administrator (RHIA). This information is available at the professional organization of the American Health Information Management Association (AHIMA.org). While there is some overlap in the field of health informatics, because the record is electronic and these professional roles complement the field of health informatics, they are not the focus of this book. **Example of what you might do in this field:** *A RHIA professional may develop the HIPAA privacy and security protocol for the archiving of medical records in the hospital system.*

how to use data, information and knowledge to solve problems in a variety of contexts. Specific to healthcare, informatics focuses on improving human health and the delivery of healthcare services (AMIA 2023) through a range of complementary informatics disciplines, falling under the umbrella of biomedical informatics. **Any number of job roles can be a part of each of these areas of informatics, including analysts, project managers, liaisons, trainers, informaticists, etc. It is important to appreciate that many similarly phrased job roles exist within all of these specialties and may differ by employer type** (e.g., outpatient clinic vs. medical insurance company vs. information technology company).

Faiola and Holden's (2017) model (Figure 1.2) demonstrates how health informatics is a derivative of biomedical informatics (BMI). As we move from biomedical informatics to types of health informatics, methods and research related to the

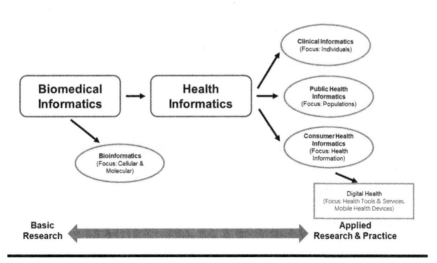

Figure 1.2 Modification of Health Informatics in Context.

Source: Faiola and Holden (2017)

field become more applied and incorporated with practice. According to Faiola and Holden's model, health informatics incorporates three areas: 1) clinical informatics, 2) public health informatics and 3) consumer health informatics. This further branches into digital health and includes categories such as mobile health applications, health IT, wearable devices, telehealth and telemedicine and personalized medicine (FDA 2020). Many of the job opportunities we describe in this book fall into these three categories.

1.4 Job Outlook

As we mentioned earlier in this chapter, health informatics is not one thing. Consequently, health informatics includes multiple job roles across multiple settings. This interdisciplinary field leverages specialties across information and social science, analytics, technology and healthcare. Therefore, jobs in health informatics don't reside in only one place. Instead, they can be found across interrelated sectors in hospitals, post-acute and nursing care settings, technology, payer systems, government, consulting and startup businesses. These include jobs in computer science, data science, analytics, healthcare, public health and information technology. There are important contributions to make and work to be done in health informatics in all of these sectors. So, for those seeking new opportunities in this field, it is important to consider the setting in which you'd like to be working.

1.5 Growth Rate

Overall, health informatics related job roles have a strong job outlook. The projected growth rate for 2019–2029 among these types of jobs is 25%, well above the average of 4% among all other occupations (see Table 1.3, Bureau of Labor

Statistics 2022a). Technological advancements, analytics to improve clinical care and the potential for predictive analytics continue to pave the way for job growth in health informatics. Additionally, job opportunities will become available based on gaps to be filled by those retiring, with roughly 25% of the workforce described as part of the baby boomer group (Pew Research 2018).

1.6 Compensation

Compensation for health informatics jobs varies widely across the spectrum of jobs in the field based on role title, skill, experience and geographical location (e.g., Midwest vs. more metropolitan city), non-profit, public hospital, etc., and whether it is an entry-level or an advanced or senior role. For example, according to Salary.com (accessed September 2022), the average pay for a clinical analyst is $70,600, and that of a data analyst is around $67,500. Or, according to ZipRecruiter.com, a clinical informatics specialist salary averages $115,500 nationally, but is estimated at $95,800 in Ohio (accessed December 2022).

According to the Bureau of Labor Statistics (BLS), related digital health job roles also vary in salary. The job role of medical and health services manager is expected to experience an overall 32% job growth between 2019 and 2029, with an average annual salary of just over $104,000, and higher average salary for the job role within certain job sectors (i.e., $159,470 in health/medical insurance industry vs. $96,570 for the role within nursing and residential care facilities). This role typically requires a minimum of a bachelor's degree and around 5 years of experience (BLS, 2022b). Executive roles in biomedical informatics require advanced experience, education and credentials and report higher compensation, among physicians in particular, but included informaticians and researchers, with a group median salary of $165,000 (range $111,000 to $230,000).

A compensation survey conducted annually by the Healthcare Information and Management Systems Society (HIMSS 2018) showed the average salary of digital health professionals in 2018 as $109,610. This number tends to be higher in vendor or health IT company settings (e.g., average of $126,910, and many jobs have bonus opportunities), followed by hospitals ($108,754), then other types of organizations ($102,316) and non-acute care settings ($99,345).

The Bureau of Labor Statistics does not currently have a specific job category for "health informatics," but Table 1.3 summarizes a set of related roles in information science, analysis and management in healthcare, related to informatics roles across different work settings. Data from these categories demonstrate not only the strong growth rate and salaries of health informatics jobs but the variety of options in work settings. Other related jobs in health informatics can include health technologists and technicians, computer and mathematical occupations and computer and information systems managers. Here is listed a description of the jobs used in the BLS analysis, depicted in Table 1.2.

TIP: Search for jobs using one of the following job titles in combination with health, healthcare or health informatics.

Description of jobs used in BLS analysis:

Computer and Information Systems Managers: Plan, direct or coordinate activities in such fields as electronic data processing, information systems, systems analysis and computer programming. Excludes "Computer Occupations."

Computer and Mathematical Occupations: Computer Systems Analysts; Information Security Analysts; Computer and Information Research Scientists; Computer Network Support Specialists; Computer User Support Specialists; Computer Network Architects; Network and Computer Systems Administrators; Database

Table 1.2 Related Job Roles in Health Informatics from U.S. Bureau of Labor Statistics

Job Sector	Computer And Information Systems Managers		Computer And Mathematical Occupations		Health Technologists And Technicians		Medical And Health Services Managers	
	Annual Average Wage 2021	Forecasted Job Growth, % (2019–2029)	Annual Mean Wage 2021	Forecasted Job Growth, % (2019–2029)	Annual Mean Wage 2021	Forecasted Job Growth, % (2019–2029)	Annual Mean Wage 2021	Forecasted Job Growth, % (2019–2029)
Direct Health And Medical Insurance Carriers	$158,220	16.7%	$97,940	19.9%	$56,500	15.4%	$168,680	40.0%
Healthcare And Social Assistance	$139,260	12.2%	$79,920	11.8%	$53,030	10.5%	$115,070	34.1%
Ambulatory Healthcare Services	$143,460	17.9%	$79,720	18.5%	$50,460	15.0%	$110,290	39.4%
Offices Of Other Health Practitioners	$141,840	26.9%	$62,630	24.6%	$$41,460	22.8%	$94,960	54.4%
Outpatient Care Centers	$143,790	19.8%	$84,220	21.6%	$55,090	19.6%	$117,340	43.7%
Hospitals (Overall)	$143,340	7.1%	$83,660	6.9%	$56,440	7.5%	$128,870	29.3%

(Continued)

Table 1.2 Related Job Roles in Health Informatics from U.S. Bureau of Labor Statistics (Continued)

Job Sector	Computer And Information Systems Managers		Computer And Mathematical Occupations		Health Technologists And Technicians		Medical And Health Services Managers	
	Annual Average Wage 2021	Forecasted Job Growth, % (2019–2029)	Annual Mean Wage 2021	Forecasted Job Growth, % (2019–2029)	Annual Mean Wage 2021	Forecasted Job Growth, % (2019–2029)	Annual Mean Wage 2021	Forecasted Job Growth, % (2019–2029)
Psychiatric And Substance Abuse Hospitals (Overall)	$102,450	14.2%	$70,750	12.8%	$41,040	12.1%	$113,130	39.0%
Specialty (Except Psychiatric And Substance Abuse) Hospitals (Overall)	$154,230	25.6%	$98,760	25.2%	$57,070	29.0%	$130,420	55.5%
Nursing And Residential Care Facilities	$110,830	12.7%	$61,690	10.1%	$51,160	5.3%	$91,760	29.3%

Job Sector	Computer And Information Systems Managers		Computer And Mathematical Occupations		Health Technologists And Technicians		Medical And Health Services Managers	
	Annual Average Wage 2021	*Forecasted Job Growth, % (2019–2029)*	*Annual Mean Wage 2021*	*Forecasted Job Growth, % (2019–2029)*	*Annual Mean Wage 2021*	*Forecasted Job Growth, % (2019–2029)*	*Annual Mean Wage 2021*	*Forecasted Job Growth, % (2019–2029)*
Residential Intellectual And Developmental Disability, Mental Health, And Substance Abuse Facilities	$106,350	19.2%	$58,700	18.5%	$41,590	20.7%	$84,080	42.6%
Social Assistance	$110,370	22.2%	$63,140	21.8%	$43,770	30.0%	$90,150	56.6%
Individual And Family Services	$114,780	30.4%	$64,400	29.9%	$43,960	33.5%	$89,910	59.8%
Average Projected Growth Rate	18.74%		18.47%		18.45%		43.64%	
Average Projected Growth Rate Across Sectors	24.83%							

Reference: BLS 2022a
Employment growth: https://data.bls.gov/projections/nationalMatrix?queryParams=5100008&ioType=i

Administrators and Architects; Computer Programmers; Software Developers and Software Quality Assurance Analysts and Testers; Web Developers and Digital Interface Designers; Computer Occupations, All Other; Actuaries; Mathematicians; Operations Research Analysts; Statisticians; Data Scientists and Mathematical Science Occupations, All Other.

Health Technologists and Technicians: All health technologists and technicians not listed separately.

Medical and Health Services Managers: Plan, direct or coordinate medical and health services in hospitals, clinics, managed care organizations, public health agencies or similar organizations.

1.7 Job Titles

You must think beyond the job title, and in some cases the description. That is because the knowledge, skills and abilities of health informatics-trained professionals can be addressed without using "health informatics" in the job description. What do we mean by that? We mean that there will be skills and competencies listed that align with the health informatics training, but they might not use the phrase "health informatics." The job description may list required and preferred skills in data analysis, human-centered design, user experience, health information systems, research, or clinical workflows. The job may also emphasize the ability to communicate well to a wide variety of stakeholders, ability to organize data, data visualization, data cleaning, integration, implementation, change management, etc. It is important for the job applicant to use keyword searches for jobs, not exclusively anchoring in the word of "informatics". There will, of course, be job descriptions for informaticist, clinical informaticist, etc. but there will be plenty of jobs listed focusing on key skills and knowledge areas for those trained in health informatics. These include: business analyst, product owner/manager, HEDIS analyst, LIMS analyst/manager, data analyst, health IT or EHR implementation manager, health IT project manager, chief medical information officer, database manager, data integration specialist, data migration specialist, EHR / EMR liaison, health information specialist, etc. (see list from BLS.gov 2022).

1.8 Job Classifications

Yes, there are many traditional full-time employee or "FTE" jobs out there. However, they are not *all* in that classification. There are options for job seekers providing opportunities to join organizations with some potential flexibility. Your job may be structured in a number of ways: full-time, part-time or a contract. It is important to clarify the job specifics when you are looking. There are a significant number of health IT services in hospitals, pharmacies or government agencies that are outsourced to consulting firms or contractors. These can be short-term projects, such as reports or program evaluations, or longer-term implementations of new software (for instance, the new EMR for the VA). These projects can be complex based on the scale, regulations and time projections related to the goals. While many contractors list jobs available, you may be working for a company that intends to bid on a job or draft a Request for Proposal (RFP) or bidding process up front. Most firms that work on government contracts have experts and templates which can help to smooth this process.

1.9 Direct Employment vs. Contracting

Many health informatics jobs are accessed as full- or part-time work directly at the company itself. That is, you'd apply to a full- or part-time job at the company in which you are interested. Still, other ways to work in the job capacity can be found through contracting agencies that already have a working contract with health information companies. Roles in these companies are organized through contracting companies for short-term or longer-term durations. This can be an option for the job candidate to indicate on their LinkedIn or other job site platform, to indicate that they are "open to contract work." In this capacity, the applicant could be an employee of the contract organization. Health information companies would then contract with the employee firm to be brought on for short- or long-term projects. On this track, you might find the job listing on a mainstream job website, but for roles driven by the contracting site (e.g., Turnberry, Apex, Genesis, etc.) may lead the interview and hiring process. Once you are hired, it would then be as a short-term or long-term contractor or consultant. Typically, you would be an employee of the contracting company. Contracts can be of various lengths, typically ranging from 30 days to one year. Contracts may or may not be renewed or extended. Contract employees may also be hired by the health information company itself, after the contract itself comes to an end.

Benefits of working as a contractor include flexibility to try new roles and companies without a long commitment to one. Moreover, contractors typically make a higher hourly rate than they would likely be paid as a full-time employee. Drawbacks include limited benefits like health insurance, retirement plan or bonus/stock option opportunities. Some contracting umbrella companies may make some benefits available, but at a higher expense to buy in. Additionally, a contractor is typically not paid for any vacation, sick time or holidays. Still, advantages to this option include flexibility and may allow a job seeker to enter the job more quickly to begin getting experience right away.

1.10 Rationale for Expanded Job Opportunities

As we write this book, we are three years past the initial onslaught of the Covid-19 global pandemic, and currently experiencing the advent of viral variants that again are challenging individuals, healthcare and long-term care settings. What we have seen since the pandemic is an increase in the need for stakeholders to be informed of the latest and most accurate information about the spread of Covid and its variants, other contagious or pervasive health threats, immunization information and patient health status. Health informaticists play an important part in facilitating this information in a timely way, in order to inform the best care plans and decision making. As healthcare continues to rely upon health IT to evaluate health status, costs and well-being of patients, roles in health informatics will continue to grow.

1.11 A Changing Workforce

Information technology has traditionally been dominated by men in everything from software developers to chief information officers. Some studies have found this as a result of "hiring people like you" rather than those who might build a more diverse workforce (Forbes 2018). While this is changing, women and people of color still face some challenges in hiring and promotions. Unfortunately, this has also been the case in health IT, with the exception of nurses entering clinical informatics roles. A study done by the Sloan School of Management at MIT found that in one high-tech company attempting to increase diversity, only 8% of its technical employees were racial minorities (MIT 2021). At the same time, there are new initiatives to make health IT more inclusive, including special-interest groups for women in health informatics (AMIA 2022) and innovation and certificate programs in informatics at Historically Black Colleges (HIMSS 2021).

Demographic shifts are influencing who is working in the health informatics workforce. Despite delays in retirement stemming from the 2008 recession, the silver tsunami of retirement will have a long-lasting impact on employment sectors (Minemyer 2018). About 70% of the Baby Boomer generation in the U.S. will be at retirement age by 2030 (Heimlich 2010). These numbers fostered a workforce shortage, even before the Covid-19 pandemic. The global pandemic exacerbated and sped up the wave of baby boomer retirements (Pandey 2021). These many retirements have exposed a void to be filled, especially in the health information technology and healthcare industry. The Gen X, Gen Z and Millennial generations are in a position to help fill gaps left by retirees in health informatics. They are particularly well positioned as most are digital natives and have been exposed to digital technology throughout the course of their lives. Employers across all sectors of health informatics job roles, including health IT, public health, payers, senior care and healthcare systems need to modify recruiting efforts to attract this younger, highly skilled workforce. This will help to accelerate digital transformation in health informatics roles.

1.12 Working Remotely

Another change in work settings for those in health informatics is the opportunity for remote work. This expanded during the Covid-19 pandemic and will likely be more common in the future. While some IT departments in health systems were already separate from the main hospital, working from home with video meetings has become more common. Some work arrangements are now characterized as hybrid, requiring some in-office days combined with some remote. Other jobs may require some travel, either within the area or longer distances. Not all companies have required employees to return to the physical building. However, EMR vendor Epic has required all employees to be on campus full-time since late 2021. Although this kind of co-location requirement is growing, overall, many companies still allow employees to work remotely. Many organizations will continue to prioritize face-to-face meetings particularly with customers, such as medical staff in the clinical setting. Still, now and into the future, these will be augmented by virtual meetings allowing for more convenience with the ongoing expansion of remote work.

1.13 Personality Profile of a Job

As you look through various job roles and their associated required skills and projected responsibilities, you begin to understand the personality profile for job roles in this area. For instance, there are jobs which require regular interaction with customers and teams to implement technology successfully. One example is a product owner or product manager who must obtain requirements from customers (for instance, a clinical team that will use the technology solution) and meet with technologists and vendors on a regular basis to meet timelines. In fact, many informatics roles act as a liaison between clinical and technical teams, so the person in this role needs to be comfortable communicating with people in these areas. On the other hand, there are those who are in what is referred to as "heads-down" roles which are more solitary, such as software developers, cybersecurity analysts and infrastructure engineers. Yet in all health informatics jobs, a degree of teamwork is required. As you review and consider various job roles and paths, consider the types of work you will be required to perform and whether that aligns with your strengths and areas you enjoy.

1.14 Changing Roles

Traditional job roles in health informatics are evolving at all levels across disciplines and stakeholder groups. A National Academy of Medicine (2022) report discusses the workforce needs of the future to support digitally enabled health will require basic competency on core organizational applications, data management, interoperability, statistics, data science, data governance, collaboration, ethics, process improvement and implementation science (Abernathy et al. 2022). Many jobs in health informatics include positions involved with the collection, handling and processing of healthcare information for a variety of purposes, from billing to improving clinical care. Accurate coding of patient records is fundamental to the entire healthcare system, both to providing treatment and ensuring providers are compensated by payers. While these are essential functions, they are only a starting point to the job growth in health informatics. Jobs related to the functional aspects of getting the right information to the right people (e.g., clinicians, patients or caregivers) at the right time to inform the best healthcare decisions will persist. Health informatics-related cybersecurity job roles are growing amidst the volumes of health data we are generating, utilizing and protecting. The practical aspects and unique skill sets will continue to diversify and grow in the coming years relative to the evolving technology that supports those functional aspects.

1.15 Diverse Skill Sets Needed

Jobs in health informatics draw upon diverse skill sets and backgrounds, including verbal and written communication, analytical skills, workflow management, clinical experience, project management, problem solving, working individually and working in teams. HIMSS (2023) discusses core competencies of health informatics, including ethical and legal issues, systems life cycle management, medical technology and management. These job opportunities in health informatics have continued to grow based on, in part, the value and meaning they have created for hospitals. Hospitals and providers need a skilled workforce in health informatics to build, integrate and use digital health tools to improve care outcomes and to decrease burden on clinicians. Stakeholders need informaticians to analyze and report on the data they collect for regulatory agencies, insurance companies and other quality control mechanisms. Health informatics professionals are working within all stakeholder groups to improve current quality while planning for the future by using innovation, effective communication and predictive analytics to improve strategies for quality of care.

1.16 International

Many health informatics work settings, companies and organizations recruit talented employees from both U.S. and international markets. Organizations using, developing and maintaining health information technology (health IT) may be familiar with hiring people on work visas or H-1B visas. If you are applying for these jobs, keep in mind that they may look for both technical and language proficiency in their hiring process.

1.17 Diversity, Equity and Inclusion

Health informatics work settings and organizations in general seek to employ the best and most talented employees. As a result, they employ people from diverse backgrounds including women, people of color and the LGBTQ+ community. In an effort to improve company culture, many health informatics related companies have created diversity, equity and inclusion (DEI) initiatives.

Health Informatics Work Settings/Ecosystems

1.18 Hospitals and Healthcare Systems

Understanding the complex healthcare ecosystem in the U.S. is the basis for getting one's head around how informatics supports these systems. In the past, the ecosystem was centralized in large and community hospitals with most physicians in solo or small group practices. Today, through mergers and consolidation, large healthcare systems have become regional or national brands composed of dozens of hospitals, medical practices, surgery centers and more. Primary care practices can be seen as feeders to specialists, including surgeons and proceduralists as well as cancer centers within the system. Integrated technology platforms including Electronic Health Records, supply chain management and customer relationship management, to mention a few, have become key to the success of large health systems.

1.19 Health Information Technology: Innovation and Consumer Health

Software and hardware developers for healthcare are an important stakeholder in the health informatics work setting ecosystem, incorporating technology, innovations and consumer health. These are the developers of electronic health records (EHR), clinical decision support (CDS) tools, medical devices, health monitors for home, mobile apps, wearables, etc. These teams of specialists incorporate many different types of professionals from software engineers to customer support to analysts. Consumer health organizations (e.g., CVS Health, Walmart) are continuing to expand in terms of engaging patients as consumers and bringing healthcare information and services to them. Health informaticists may have many roles available to them in these companies as business analysts, project managers, product owners, clinical liaisons with hospital partners, user experience specialists, knowledge managers and beyond.

1.20 Health Insurance/Payer Organizations

Insurance providers are another large user of health IT services. Payers can be national, regional or confined to a specific state; some are sponsored by health systems or self-insured companies. Claims processing has become more efficient as it has moved to paperless. Analytics of the vast amount of data has enabled insurers to predict risk and create pricing algorithms. Annual enrollment and provider contracting are other systems that are supported by IT. Some insurers have also become providers and have acquired EHRs and other clinical systems which require support. Health Maintenance Organizations, such as Kaiser Permanente, have been insurance providers and medical systems for many years.

1.21 Consulting

Consulting in health informatics has been a key part of the ecosystem. Large firms, such as Gartner, EY and Deloitte have significant healthcare practices advising health IT leadership. Many combine market research reports and surveys with their consulting services. Smaller consulting firms are more likely to be boutique practices focusing on specialty areas, such as cybersecurity, digital transformation or supply chain.

1.22 Long-Term Care/Senior Care

Long-term care, home care, behavioral health and rehabilitation centers are the next setting of focus. These can be attached to health systems, national chains or independent organizations. They can be not-for-profit or for-profit groups. They primarily do post-acute care or long-term care in a facility or in the home. New trends include telemedicine and hospital-at-home, which can include multiple technologies to support severely ill patients or ongoing chronic care which may require remote monitoring support. Health informatics roles help senior and aging service organizations to capture or share health information with their own staff or with accessing hospital, provider, pharmacy or laboratory patient information. Roles tend to focus on regulatory and quality reporting, as well as maintaining or establishing interoperability of records. For example, a patient at a long-term care facility who falls and needs to be transferred to a hospital for acute care can be tracked in the hospital's electronic system. Eventually the patient is discharged back to the long-term care facility. The informatics challenge is how staff can get their hospital care records back to the long-term care facility's records system. With this information (i.e., through a summary of care) about any tests or procedures the patient received, there is a better chance of not repeating the test, making it less expensive and less of a hardship for the older adults.

1.23 Government

A number of government agencies at national, state and local levels engage in health IT. On the national level, the Office of the National Coordinator for Health IT (ONC), part of Health and Human Services (HHS), engages in policy and regulations related to health informatics. The Centers for Medicare and Medicaid Services (CMS) has an Innovation Center which experiments with new reimbursement models and health IT innovations. The

Food and Drug Administration (FDA) regulates medical devices including those used in digital health. The Veterans Health Administration (VA) was an early adopter of EMRs and is in the process of moving from a homegrown system to a major vendor product. On the state and local levels, there is some health informatics activity in policy development and implementation, particularly around Medicaid and Health Information Exchanges (HIEs).

1.24 How This Book Is Organized

Now that we have described the current job market and emerging demographic changes in the workforce, we will outline the sections of this book. Next, we will examine career opportunities in the six identified healthcare settings or ecosystems: 1) hospitals and healthcare systems, 2) health information technology, 3) health insurance or payer organizations, 4) consulting, 5) long-term care or senior care and 6) government. In particular, we will look at healthcare settings where patients and clinicians are. We will look at healthcare information technology in detail, including jobs in software development, medical equipment and mobile devices. We will examine jobs with payers or insurance companies, including those with private insurance companies and government agencies. In addition, we will explore careers in research, policy and professional organizations related to health informatics. One of the fastest-growing areas is health informatics innovation. The emergence of entrepreneurs and innovation centers offers opportunities not only in startup companies but also for consultants. We will then review studies in the field of health informatics. This includes learning about what the professional organizations are communicating about career paths in health informatics. We will conclude with an overview of career phases and next steps describing how to make changes today to enhance career and professional development through involvement and leadership.

References

Abernathy, Amy, Laura Adams, Meredith Barrett, Christine Bechtel, Patricia Brennan, Atul Butte, Judith Faulkner, Elaine Fontaine, Stephen Friedhoff, John Halamka, and Michael Howell. "The Promise of Digital Health: Then, Now, and the Future." *NAM Perspectives* 6, no. 22 (2022). https://doi.org/10.31478/202206e.

Admin. "What Is Nursing Informatics?" *HIMSS*, March 25, 2021. www.himss.org/resources/what-nursing-informatics.

"AHIMA." *AHIMA Salary Survey Report: HIM Professionals in 2019*, 2019. www.ahima.org/media/betc41er/salary-snapshot.pdf.

American Nurses Association (ANA). *Nursing Informatics: Scope and Standards of Practice*. Washington, DC: American Nurses Association, 2014.

"Amia Salary Survey: American Medical Informatics Association." *AMIA*, 2018. https://amia.org/.

Bayat, Ardeshir. "Bioinformatics" (2002). *BMJ*. Apr 27; 324(7344): 1018–1022. doi: 10.1136/bmj.324.7344.1018

Blash, Anthony. "Pharmacy Informatics and Its Cross-Functional Role in Healthcare." *HIMSS*, September 20, 2021. https://www.himss.org/resources/pharmacy-informatics-and-its-cross-functional-role-healthcare.

Center for Devices and Radiological Health. "What Is Digital Health?" *U.S. Food and Drug Administration, FDA*, September 22, 2020. www.fda.gov/medical-devices/digital-health-center-excellence/what-digital-health.

Faiola, Anthony, and Richard J. Holden. "Consumer Health Informatics: Empowering Healthy-Living-Seekers Through Mhealth." *Progress in Cardiovascular Diseases* 59, no. 5 (2017): 479–86. https://doi.org/10.1016/j.pcad.2016.12.006.

Fry, Richard. "Millennials Are the Largest Generation in the U.S. Labor Force." *Pew Research Center*, April 11, 2018. www.pewresearch.org/fact-tank/2018/04/11/millennials-largest-generation-us-labor-force/.

Giles, Kimberly. "Council Post: Why You Mistakenly Hire People Just Like You." *Forbes Magazine*, May 1, 2018. www.forbes.com/sites/forbescoachescouncil/2018/05/01/why-you-mistakenly-hire-people-just-like-you/?sh=4/b92b3b3827.

"Health Information 101." *AHIMA*, 2022. https://www.ahima.org/certification-careers/certifications-overview/career-tools/career-pages/health-information-101/.

Heimlich, Russell. "Baby Boomers Retire." *Pew Research Center*, December 29, 2010. https://www.pewresearch.org/fact-tank/2010/12/29/baby-boomers-retire/.

HIMSS, Health Informatics Guide, by Toria Shaw Morawski, Johannes Thye, Marisa L. Wilson, and Hank Fanberg (2023); https://www.himss.org/resources/health-informatics#:~:text=This%20multidisciplinary%20field%20exists%20at,services%20delivery%2C%20management%20and%20planning; accessed May 30, 2023.

"HIMSS 2018 US Compensation Survey." *2018 HIMSS U.S. Compensation Survey*, 2018. www.himss.org/sites/hde/files/d7/u132196/2018_HIMSS_US_Compensation_Survey_Final_Report.pdf.

"Informatics: Research and Practice." *AMIA – American Medical Informatics Association*, 2023. https://amia.org/about-amia/why-informatics/informatics-research-and-practice.

Kulikowski, Casimir A., Edward H. Shortliffe, Leanne M. Currie, Peter L. Elkin, Lawrence E. Hunter, Todd R. Johnson, Ira J. Kalet, Leslie A. Lenert, Mark A. Musen, Judy G. Ozbolt, Jack W. Smith, Peter Z. Tarczy-Hornoch, and Jeffrey J. Williamson. "AMIA Board White Paper: Definition of Biomedical Informatics and Specification of Core Competencies for Graduate Education in the Discipline." *Journal of the American Medical Informatics Association* 19, no. 6 (2012): 931–38. https://doi.org/10.1136/amiajnl-2012-001053.

"May 2021 OEWS National Industry-Specific Occupational Employment and Wage Estimates." *U.S. Bureau of Labor Statistics*, March 31, 2022a. www.bls.gov/oes/current/oessrci.htm#62.

"Medical and Health Services Managers: Occupational Outlook Handbook." *U.S. Bureau of Labor Statistics*, October 25, 2022b. www.bls.gov/ooh/management/medical-and-health-services-managers.htm.

Minemyer, Paige. "Wave of Baby Boomer Retirements Could Sap a Quarter of the Public Health Workforce." *Fierce Healthcare*, January 23, 2018. https://www.fiercehealthcare.com/healthcare/public-health-workforce-baby-boomers-retirement-american-journal-preventive-medicine.

"Morehouse School of Medicine and HIMSS Global Health Equity Network Partner to Innovate Health Informatics Programs." *HIMSS*, June 16, 2021. www.himss.org/news/morehouse-school-medicine-and-himss-global-health-equity-network-partner-innovate-health.

"National Employment Matrix." *U.S. Bureau of Labor Statistics.* Accessed December 7, 2022. https://data.bls.gov/projections/nationalMatrix?queryParams=510000&ioType=i.

Pandey, Erica. "Millions of Baby Boomers Retired Early during the Pandemic." *Axios,* October 29, 2021. https://www.axios.com/2021/10/29/millions-of-baby-boomers-retired-early-during-the-pandemic.

"Site Built by: Data Analyst Salary." *Salary.com.* Accessed September 2022. www.salary.com/research/salary/listing/data-analyst-salary.

"Site Built by: Clinical Analyst Salary." *Salary.com.* Accessed September 2022. www.salary.com/research/salary/posting/clinical-analyst-salary.

Somers, Meredith. "A New Barrier to Diverse Hiring in Tech." *MIT Sloan,* March 31, 2021. https://mitsloan.mit.edu/ideas-made-to-matter/a-new-barrier-to-diverse-hiring-tech.

"Understanding Health Informatics Core Competencies." *HIMSS,* 2023. https://www.himss.org/resources/health-informatics.

"Women in AMIA." *Affinity Group.* Accessed December 7, 2022. https://amia.org/communities/women_in_amia.

Chapter 2

Getting the Job

This chapter offers perspectives from experienced professionals about strategies for getting a job in health informatics. First, we discuss the experience you bring as a job candidate. Next, we look at how health informatics is evolving in the 21st century, along with changing and newer job categories. Then, we examine an innovation mindset for careers in health informatics. Lastly, we offer a strategy on your approach to applying for a job, as well as a recommendation for three competency areas to emphasize as you position yourself for a new career in the field.

2.1 Do I Need Clinical Experience to Get a Job in Health Informatics?

Having different backgrounds and experiences is a strength and makes for a unique candidate. There are some jobs that require clinical experience, such as a nursing informatics specialist, but there are also jobs that do not require clinical experience, such as health informatics specialists, data analysts

DOI: 10.4324/9781003185727-2

and integration managers. This field allows for a wide variety of backgrounds.

Do you need to be a nurse? Or a doctor? A pharmacist? The short answer is no. That said, there are some jobs that specify their requirement to be a clinician. You will need to find the answer to this in each job category when you are interested in a certain job, because the titles for both categories can be very similar (e.g., clinical informatics specialist). Find out the requirements before you proceed. Informatics roles in these organizations vary but tend to include both clinical and non-clinical roles. That is, some jobs are listed as nursing informatics, medical informatics or pharmacy informatics, all of which require a specified corresponding clinical degree (being a nurse, physician or pharmacist). Other job titles (e.g., clinical or health informatics specialist, integrations manager, data analyst, product manager, etc.) do not require clinical training or licensure. Look closely at job descriptions to note this requirement or lack thereof.

2.2 How Can I Leverage my Clinical Experience?

While it is not needed in many health informatics roles, having a clinical background is an asset. If you've been working as a clinician, you can transition to the health informatics sector. Your subject matter expertise of healthcare and the clinical care setting adds value to many informatics roles. For example, your perspective is critical at a health IT, innovation or consumer health information organization. You know how patients, fellow clinicians, co-workers and caregivers navigate in a given setting, what they find helpful and valuable, and on the flip side, what they find problematic or painful. These types of insights, coupled with your training in informatics, make you a valuable candidate in health informatics.

2.3 What If I Have No Clinical or Healthcare Experience?

How about non-clinicians? If you have been working as an analyst or technical consultant in a different field from healthcare, you can still be a good candidate for a job in a health IT organization. Your expertise and experience in analytics, project management, change management, databases, communicating across different stakeholder groups, combined with your informatics background help to position you as a great candidate for an informatics career. It is important to articulate your domain expertise, your skills (technical and soft skills) and your ability to manage a project individually or with a group. Convey how you help the group to solve problems using health information and technology.

2.4 What If I'm Making a Career Change?

Just because you have never worked in healthcare does not mean that you cannot apply your technical and business savvy in health informatics roles. Pratt (2022) reports the Computer Programs and Systems, Inc. (CPSI) chief innovation officer, Wes Cronkite, as saying that their company will take on great technology talent even if they don't have healthcare experience.

Employees and applicants with a health informatics background will use skills in data and information to empower healthcare and life sciences leaders to make decisions from healthcare data that may be from disparate and varying places. In order to help organizations in an informatics role, it is important to communicate with clients and stakeholders to understand the problems to solve. Based on the solution, it is important to help identify the right data, access it, analyze and interpret it and help stakeholders to utilize it for decision making. Beyond these functions, employees or applicants who have skill in data storage and data security are essential. This is fueled by the need for healthcare organizations and related entities to securely maintain data, and make it intuitive and easy to access for those with the appropriate security clearance. Ransomware attacks on hospitals continue to rise, with 66% of healthcare organizations attacked in 2021, up from 34% in 2020 (Berry 2022). People in cybersecurity job roles in health information are doing meaningful work and will continue to be a requirement of the organization. So, you can see that a number of skills can be quite valuable for the organization, including good communication, organization, technical skills, knowledge of regulations and standards related to interoperability, reporting and technology integration.

2.5 What If I Am a New Graduate and Don't Have Much Experience?

For those of you with an informatics or related degree but very little work experience, never fear! Many health information companies are hiring recent graduates. Major health IT companies (e.g., EHR vendors), insurance companies, long-term care or hospital systems hire people with degrees and a history of academic excellence or professional success. The bottom line is that these companies want to hire people who can learn quickly, can problem solve independently or in a group and who can communicate well with other stakeholders in the business. As a new graduate, there are many entry-level positions in health informatics that you can start with and learn and advance in the business from there.

2.6 New and Changing Jobs in Health Informatics

Work roles in health informatics continue to evolve. For example, we can now find job announcements for "senior faculty of quantum computing research" at the Cleveland Clinic. This position in quantum computing simply did not exist 10 years ago. However, because of advancements in technology and computational techniques, we now have quantum comput–ing and with it the potential benefits of enhanced, multi-dimensional, predictive and rapid analysis of any number of big data sets in healthcare including medical images, genomics, medicine, chemistry, pharmaceuticals, epidemiology or public health. This is just one example. There will be other techno-logical advancements, yet unnamed, that will be aligned with informatics roles in the future. A health informaticist will con-tinue to find ways to improve health and healthcare through data and information with the technology available at the time.

Although system architecture is not a new field, it is applied in a novel way in healthcare. The health information systems across the specialty areas of healthcare continue to change and need to be interoperable with other systems. For example, a hospital may have a best-in-class lab system, but their primary EHR vendor has an updated application and they now want to change to the EHR vendor's lab product because of integration ease and cost savings. Because of this, job roles emerge for sys-tem architects in a variety of different areas, such as laboratory, pharmacy and nutrition systems. Thus, we need health infor-maticians who can participate and add value in not only these growing areas, but also have foresight and flexibility for aspects of health informatics job roles on the horizon.

We see this currently in the use of artificial intelligence, machine learning and mixed reality technologies. These are still relatively new technologies, and health informatics special-ists are working with these tools in their work across job roles (i.e., data analysts, clinical informaticians, EHR liaisons, trainers, etc.). As digital health tools evolve and emerge, we will need informaticists who can understand, clean, prepare, and use the data these tools supply to improve health and healthcare. Health informaticians' roles will remain foundational in healthcare. Technological innovations will continue, whether it is through mobile devices or quantum computers, and informaticians' work will need to align.

2.7 Innovation as a Strategy

As you look at job opportunities in this sector, it is important to keep in mind that innovation is essential across the landscape of businesses and organizations developing products and services to address market needs. Among health information technology organizations, innovation is often part of the strategy, resulting in jobs in product development through specialized departments or innovation centers. These companies can range from small startups to large multinational corporations focused on biotechnology, bioscience, healthcare, or consumer health products, supply chain, wellness and related services. Many startup healthcare technology companies can align with state-based jobs initiatives (e.g., www.jobsohio.com/industries/healthcare/) or technology incubators sponsored by private equity groups, universities, NGOs, non-profit research centers, companies or government agencies (regional, state, national and international). These companies are based all over the world and compete for people with the skill sets to help them achieve their goals.

Innovation divisions of larger companies may have a stand-alone or affiliated innovation center or department. These groups may exist as spin-off entities whose sole mission is to develop minimum viable products (MVP) to test in the market and develop for further use. These innovations can be for both internal (co-workers and divisions of the larger company) and external (clients or customers) stakeholders. Innovative solutions can take the form of updates in software, modified or streamlined hardware or wearables, among others. Solutions will incorporate your domain expertise, technical skills, soft skills and ability to complete a project.

2.8 Innovation Mindset

Skills development and innovation are part of the strategic approach for many of these organizations. Thus, any person interested in working for these organizations should have not only a solid set of skills aligned with company interests, but also the right philosophical approach to continue enhancing their skill sets as time goes on. The mindset is one of continuous improvement and learning. Technology evolves, and so should the employees who leverage it to help achieve goals. A "fail fast or learn quickly" philosophy is typically embraced in an innovation culture, including health information technology companies.

For job applicants in health informatics, it is a highly sought-after skill to find talent that can bridge the gap between or be the translator between the clinician's experience and the technology specialists or developers. Dr. Shauna Overgaard at Mayo Clinic, discussed the critical function of translational informaticists in the symbiotic relationship between data scientists and clinicians. That is, informaticists play a pivotal role in enabling data scientists by facilitating their comprehension of the clinical team's requirements, workflows, and contextual situations. Simultaneously, informaticists strive to ensure that the clinical team acquires a comprehensive understanding of the functional aspects of data science. Tyler Allchin, Managing Director of Healthcare for JobsOhio forecasts that the next healthcare frontier is at the intersection of technology, data and healthcare. Specifically, there is a need for an understanding of genomic data, biotechnology, electronic health records, health information and bloodwork data as it is integrated with healthcare workflows. Health information technology and innovation-based companies are seeking job applicants who can solve problems and improve health and healthcare using data and information.

This does not mean the job applicant needs to have mastered all skills the company could ever want, but instead, to have an area of proficiency or expertise (e.g., database management, data analysis, etc.) and a demonstrated ability to learn more. This could be something that you discuss in an interview. It is also demonstrated through your pursuit of education through a degree or certificate. The takeaway here is that you demonstrate that you are willing and able to learn new material and apply it, and that you approach your work life with enthusiasm and active engagement.

Throughout the domain-specific chapters of this book, you will see sections on "people skills" and "technical skills." We added these because it is important to consider all components of how you can add value to a job. These facets are both important in getting the job.

2.9 Have a Good Attitude and Be Willing to Learn

In a recent conversation with a director of data warehousing and reporting at a regional hospital, we asked what his organization is looking for when they hire new employees in the informatics division. He said that they look for skilled people who have a good attitude and are willing to learn. He reminded us that candidates will go far in life with this combination of personal characteristics. We wholeheartedly agree!

When we prepare students for internships, we encourage them to check their ego at the door, be willing to learn, and help the team to complete projects. You may not always be doing what you originally thought, but it will more than likely be worthwhile and lead to project involvement you

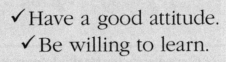

Figure 2.1   Job Coaching Advice.

would not have been able to join otherwise. A good attitude will take you far.

2.10 Practical Insights from Health Informatics Thought Leaders

Practical insights about what could help people who are seeking a career in health informatics come from those experienced industry leaders who are hiring people to fill these roles.

Mr. Ed Marx, former Chief Information Officer (CIO) at the Cleveland Clinic, notes that he prioritized his time this way: 50% with customers, 25% with peers and 25% with teams. Ed began his career managing implementation projects and taking on more responsibility managing teams. He kept his focus on what skills he would need for his ultimate goal of being CIO for a large health system. He wanted to strengthen his teams to be the best, so he encouraged them to join him in physical challenges like mountain climbing. Reaching his goal included not only people and project management but also understanding the strategic importance of health IT and how it can help meet the broader goals of the organization.

Mr. Peter Kress, CIO and Senior Vice President of Acts Retirement Life Communities, offered his advice for those

Figure 2.2   Areas of Competency for Health Informatics Jobs.

seeking to have a career in health informatics. Specifically, he identified three areas of competency for new job seekers or those making a transition to health informatics roles:

1. Develop a portfolio of **technology skills**. This can be different for each person – perhaps one person is skilled in database management while another is skilled in lab information systems – but you better have a strong portfolio. In that portfolio, you have to have a deep understanding about data (what it is, where it came from, how it is structured), data analysis (what tests would be appropriate to use to answer certain questions), and at least some knowledge of data science (how to elicit meaningful insights from the data available using various techniques, like creating an algorithm). Anybody who is using information has to understand how that information yields insight. While highlighting data, you can use development languages or application systems as well (Cerner, Epic, wearables, devices, etc.). Just be sure to discuss some technical and data expertise.

2. Demonstrate that you can **complete projects with both small and large teams.** This area will draw upon your experience with and competency in product management, project management or change management. You will need to work with teams to make projects happen, often working in an agile environment where projects are quick-paced and flexible to stakeholder feedback. This area is embedded in design thinking and innovation strategies.

Because rapid changes and solutions are being assembled, they are increasingly designed and iterated rapidly around consumer/service/improvement models. Product management skill sets such as communication and strategic thinking are a great way to anchor this whole set of competencies. At the heart of it, you need to learn how to get things done individually and as part of a team.

3. Identify your **domain expertise**. In this area, think of this less as "what is my expertise?" and instead, think about it as what you can bring to solve increasingly complex use cases. There is complexity in the field of health and well-being. Instead of focusing only on a narrow area without context, talk about your expertise and how it addresses problems. People don't build life strategies out of one narrow area. Even if you know how to develop an app or use a tool, talk about how it helps the broader context. That is, talk about how to integrate, how to coordinate experience, how to orchestrate or optimize. In order to do that, it is important to understand more deeply how people in the organization or the stakeholders express needs and engage with each other to improve and manage health. In the healthcare field, we need different domain expertise. Think about domain expertise as part of a portfolio as well. Yes, have a narrow skill, but build it out and know how that skill can help solve the bigger problem. You have to build expertise in an agile way so you are changing and adapting every day.

Mr. Kress shared that health informatics is going through a significant transition, moving to a more holistic model. That is, frameworks for treating health tend not to be simply narrow and isolated. There is a recognized continuum or spectrum from acute care to managing daily wellness. People have new strategies for thinking about their health and wellness that might incorporate accessing a personal health record from their doctor's visit to an app to help them manage their caloric intake, monitor blood sugar levels, guide a meditation or remind them to take medication. The health informatics of the future has to move rigorously to the idea of being able to describe personal well-being in as expansive a way as possible, incorporating a wide set of interdisciplinary models.

2.11 Summary

As a health informaticist, your role is about navigating the way in which technology and information inform a constantly evolving medical practice. Position yourself to get the job by clearly communicating your technical skills, domain expertise and your ability to complete projects both independently and with a group. Have a good attitude and be willing to learn new information and skills. This is not easy to do. You need to approach a new learning opportunity with humility and positivity. Be the communicator, the team player, and leader you want others to be.

Now that you have been coached into presenting yourself in the strongest way for your new job, let's examine the six work settings or ecosystems in which most health informatics jobs currently exist. The next chapters will provide an overview of job roles in hospitals, health IT organizations, health insurance companies or payers, consulting, long-term care or senior care and government.

References

Berry, Melissa D. "Ransomware Attacks Against Healthcare Organizations Nearly Doubled in 2021, Report Says." *Thomson Reuters Institute*, July 5, 2022. www.thomsonreuters.com/en-us/posts/investigation-fraud-and-risk/ransomware-attacks-against-healthcare/.

"Healthcare." *JobsOhio.* Accessed January 16, 2023. www.jobsohio. com/industries/healthcare.

Pratt, Mary K. "How to Get a Job in Healthcare IT." *Computerworld,* June 15, 2022. https://www-computerworld-com.cdn.ampproject.org/c/s/www.computerworld.com/article/3663674/how-to-get-a-job-in-healthcare-it.amp.html.

Chapter 3

Careers in Hospitals and Health Systems

"Information technology workers come to healthcare out of a desire for meaningful work, something that makes a difference."

– Ed Marx
CEO of Divurgent and formerly CIO of the Cleveland Clinic Foundation

3.1 Introduction to Hospitals and Health Systems

To understand the job roles and career paths in informatics, one must comprehend the dynamic changes in the structure and processes in healthcare. Most hospitals are now part of regional health systems which may span several states or even have an international presence. With the acquisitions and consolidations, these health systems are also acquiring group medical practices including primary care and specialty groups.

DOI: 10.4324/9781003185727-3

What does this mean for technology support? For one thing, it has meant getting on the same page for EMRs. For example, if St. John Hospital and Dr. Francis, an outpatient primary care provider (PCP), are part of the same health system but St. John is using EMR vendor A and Dr. Francis is using EMR vendor B, those EMRs will struggle to work together. Patient data will be captured and stored differently based on the different EMR set-ups. Say patient Jane Doe goes to St. John for an emergency room visit and then is discharged to follow up with her PCP, Dr. Francis. Data transfer isn't just the click of a button. Much of Jane Doe's information stored in the St. John EMR is going to need to be specifically interfaced to or manually reen-tered into Dr. Francis's EMR, or is simply lost in the transition between care settings. To meet this type of challenge, major projects can include either moving all hospitals and medi-cal practices to a single vendor system or creating their own Health Information Exchange to enable the movement of data within the system. It also has the advantage of consolidating other large systems, such as finance and supply chain.

At the same time, systems are able to create large data warehouses with huge amounts of data for analysis using both a centralized tool set and distributed systems empowering nurses and managers to query data for quality improvement, for instance. Data analytics has become a core function pro-viding reports and dashboards for public reporting, financial analysis and newer areas, such as predictive analytics.

Hospitals and health systems continue to be a highly regu-lated industry. From quality reporting to CMS and the Joint Commission to patient satisfaction and patient registries, data flow and secure storage have essential functions. The Health Insurance Portability and Accountability Act (HIPAA) deter-mines how to secure and share healthcare data held by pro-viders, although revisions to these regulations are in process. With increasing threats of hacking, ransomware and phishing attacks, cybersecurity has emerged as an essential element of this data-rich environment.

Provider workflow has become an ongoing phase 2 project around EMRs. Provider workflow here refers to how providers interact with the electronic systems in order to do their job. No provider wants to navigate through ten separate screens to get to the information they need! They want the system to be set up in a way that makes it easy for them to access the necessary data. With many complaints about how workflow is poorly structured during the initial implementation of EMRs, enhancing workflow has become a major role for Chief Medical Information Officers (CMIO) along with governance committees that determine prioritization of changes in EMR workflow to enhance provider efficiency. Another aspect of workflow is embedded clinical decision support tools (CDS). These tools include warnings about medication interactions, reminders about preventive care scheduling and order sets which standardize care, such as preparation for a procedure or surgery. While these CDS tools provide better standardization of care and patient safety, too many alerts can frustrate providers and affect workflow efficiency. Since supporting and enhancing the EMR is focused on a single vendor, health systems build teams of informaticists with certification on various modules in the vendor's EMR. Typically, staff members have multiple certifications.

On the finance side of healthcare, the systems are more complex than just generating a bill. Coding systems are needed with full teams to ensure that appropriate diagnostic and procedure codes are submitted to insurance companies. There are payer contract systems to manage the complexity of hundreds of requirements for each contracted payer. Patient-facing account systems are common now allowing patients to both view their bills and pay online. Insurance prior approval and denial systems also are prevalent in the industry.

Supply chains for everything from drugs to linens and medical technology, have drawn more attention since the Covid epidemic. Thousands of types of medical supplies are needed for hospitals and medical practices. The ready availability of medical technology is essential on a 24/7 basis, including everything from ventilators to IV pumps and glucose meters. Pharmacy systems manage large inventories as well. While most large health systems used Just-in-Time inventory systems in the past – which delivered inventory on an as-needed basis and prevented overstocking – this is being rethought based on experience from the Covid-19 epidemic shortages. Inventory databases and ordering systems as well as logistics are typically part of an enterprise system (HIMSS, 2022).

3.2 A Day in the Life

A typical day in the life of a health system informatics professional is difficult to describe because of the wide variety of roles and responsibilities. But a few scenarios will illustrate some categories of roles. For instance, some roles regularly interact with internal customers, identifying their needs to find new technologies or improve on existing technologies. A nurse informaticist would meet regularly with nurse administrators to improve nursing workflow. Similar to provider workflow as discussed earlier, this refers to helping nurses interact with electronic systems easily and efficiently. Next, they would spend time evaluating potential solutions within the existing EMR or talk to vendors about additional systems that could be embedded into the EMR to enhance workflow efficiency. To make a change in the EMR, the informaticist would need to write a proposal to the EMR governance committee documenting the specific nature of the change and the potential gains in efficiency and outcomes. They might then need to meet with the Chief Nursing Informatics Officer and the Chief Medical

Informatics Officer to request the change be prioritized. Meanwhile, they would offer continuous communication with the requesting department.

Tim Sobol previously worked as Business Relationship Manager (BRM) for the Heart and Vascular Institute at the Cleveland Clinic. Currently, he is Senior Program Manager at UC Davis Health. His daily focus is how to enhance clinical and operational efficiencies. This may include working on EMR modules to enhance specific clinical workflows, working with physicians and nurses to optimize their time utilization and at the same time improve clinical outcomes. This typically involves interdisciplinary meetings where he translates user needs into technical solutions. For example, an operating room management package requires collaboration not just with surgeons but also the OR nurses, anesthesiologist, supply chain and others to ensure interdisciplinary collaboration. He also works on introducing new digital health tools on a pilot basis with a clinical lead to determine whether they are a help or hindrance to the clinical and administrative work of the institute. He works with the cardiac imaging teams to improve the storage and movement of digital images. Some of his daily tasks may be working on purely technical projects, such as cybersecurity or enhancing data visualization tools for analysis of granular questions from clinicians. For instance, providers who have requested better data visualization for quality improvement may involve not only providing a new data management tool to be installed, but also cleaning and adding more data to the data lake being used for this purpose.

Ed Marx, former health system Chief Information Officer of the Cleveland Clinic and now the CEO of Divurgent, held many informatics roles in his career before becoming CIO at a major health system. His experience with hiring IT staff included looking at the passion the candidate had for the work, their service ethic and their ability to work as part of a team. In his career, almost half of his time was spent with customers (in the hospital, that means internal customers, both clinical and administrative), and the rest of the time with peers and teams. This meant that a typical day would be in a variety of meetings with customers wanting new products or EMR enhancements, team building meetings and activities including leadership training and mentoring and working with peers at the "C" level (CEO, CFO, etc.) and team level to move projects forward.

On the other hand, some IT staff spend more time on technical tasks. For example, programmers would spend most of their time writing code, testing it and discussing progress with their team. Someone on their team would be communicating with the group who requested this program, and discussions with teams supporting any system they would want to send data to or pull data from would need to occur on a regular basis. Something like writing a module that would use data from the EMR utilizing a FHIR standard (Fast Healthcare Interoperability Resource) would need permission from the system administrator to enable that connection. For instance, they could partner with an app that helps patients search for the lowest-cost options for their medications so that patients who opt in can have their medication list pulled into the app from the EMR.

Security professionals may also spend more time on technical tasks. This would include monitoring security systems for any breaches or invalid user accounts, evaluating and installing security software to improve the protection of clinical data. The security team would also meet regularly with each other and organizational compliance officers, and would train other IT teams and employees on security procedures.

Engineers spend time on the most technical level, whether working on data center issues, managing a cloud infrastructure, new equipment installations or enhancing the interoperability of systems.

The commonalities in the day-in-the-life experience in informatics are a combination of technical tasks, evaluating solutions and communication within teams, across IT teams and with internal customers on a regular basis.

3.3 Informatics Roles

Informatics requires multiple roles working in tandem. At the leadership level, there are typically three key positions: Chief Information Officer (CIO), Chief Medical Information Officer (CMIO) and Chief Nursing Informatics Officer (CNIO). Some institutions have added positions like Chief Technology Officer (CTO), Chief Security Officer (CSO), Chief Research Informatics Officer (CRIO), Chief Data Officer (CDO) and Chief Innovation Officer, although this last role may be broader than informatics. Some of these may be identified as vice presidents or directors under one of the first three "C-level" positions.

Under each of these leadership positions in informatics or information technology, there are typically departments including clinical informatics (may include nursing informatics), infrastructure, networks and data center, security, project management, analytics and business intelligence, training and financial systems. The individual roles/job titles in each department may be as general as system analyst (often three levels based on experience and training), project manager, product manager, data analyst, programmer or data center manager. Others might have more specialized roles or job titles related to specific products or processes, such as pharmacy informaticists, data integration specialist, network administrator or EMR training specialist.

3.3.1 Project Management

Many hospitals and health systems now have IT project management offices. These are typically staffed by certified Project Management Professionals (PMP) to implement new software or technology or manage upgrades to large systems. A newer role acknowledging the importance of internal customer relationship management – meaning managing the needs of employees rather than external customers, such as patients – is portfolio management. Evolving out of project management, this role places a senior IT employee to interface with administrators, physicians, nurses and others in a specific clinical or administrative division to understand their technology needs to improve clinical and operational efficiency. Throughout the information technology structure, teamwork is essential as any new product or upgrade will require multiple roles working together as project or portfolio manager and an executive sponsor.

3.3.2 *Infrastructure*

Maintaining information technology infrastructure requires highly trained team members. The roles involve managing the health system's data center with potentially thousands of servers, routers and backup systems in a climate-controlled building. This may include installing or replacing servers in racks, allocating space for systems, ensuring uptime and planning and practicing emergency downtime procedures. For example, a major weather event knocks out servers and nurses and providers cannot access the EMR while tech issues are being fixed. They need to continue to work and care for patients, so downtime procedures are vital. The backup system must be initiated quickly, or they will need to use paper charting for a short period of time.

3.3.3 *Network Connectivity*

Managing networking connections requires a team which usually is certified in networking devices and software, such as Cisco Certified. This team might also manage the wireless network within the organization, including a secure private network for employees and a public network for visitors. Within the infrastructure team, there is a newer role related to moving data and using data from cloud solutions. In the past, healthcare organizations chose to keep their data internal, in their own data centers. But as cloud providers have enhanced their security procedures to become HIPAA-compliant at low cost, many healthcare organizations are moving data to the cloud, including (in some cases) their EMR infrastructure. There is also a concept of a hybrid cloud, meaning that a system may have some data in the cloud and some onsite. IT infrastructure teams need staff that understands the appropriate uses of cloud providers and the best practices of moving data to and from the cloud securely.

3.3.4 Tech Support

Desktop support and support of other connected devices requires a team trained in managing desktop/laptops remotely, as well as an onsite team to do troubleshooting, replacement and new deployment of workstations.

3.3.5 Training

Training in IT systems includes a team that primarily provides onsite or remote training of existing systems or new systems. As a part of onboarding for new employees, hands-on training in the systems they will need for their job role, whether clinical or administrative, is essential. This can include training in the use of the EMR for physicians and nurses, pharmacy systems for pharmacists and pharmacy technicians, finance systems, etc. Typically, organizations have training labs with 10 or more desktop computers with the software installed to do instructor-led training. More technical or specialized training may be outsourced to education providers or provided by the software vendor.

3.3.6 Security

IT security provides a key function which is only getting more important as hackers increasingly attack hospital systems. IT security professionals are typically highly trained and certified in security procedures. This may include roles such as managing firewalls and other technology to secure enterprise systems. This team may also ensure the security of internal networks and desktops by deploying security software into these technologies and monitoring on a continuous basis. Security teams sometimes provide training in privacy and security including education about HIPAA and prevention of security breaches caused by email or social media. Security systems now typically include warning systems in the corporate email system and browser protection on desktop computers.

3.3.7 Data Management and Analytics

As mentioned, data warehouses, common in health systems, require teams with a range of skills. Teams responsible for data analytics can include data analysts who directly serve internal customers by gathering data or creating requested reports and public reporting analysts who create reports for the Joint Commission on Accreditation of Hospitals or the Centers for Medicare and Medicaid (CMS) or others. Others may have more technical roles in managing data movement like Extract, Transform and Load (ETL) processes from various sources, such as multiple EMR systems, into the single data warehouse. Still others will be involved in data standards and data providence ensuring what is referred to as a single source of truth for the data. Another part of the team would be writing computer programs or performing data science requiring more advanced training in programming and statistical analysis.

3.3.8 Research

For academic medical centers (AMCs), research is a key component of their mission. Support of this mission from informatics professionals requires some understanding of how clinical trials operate and how they are regulated. For example, software for data management of clinical trials for new drugs or devices require compliance with a Food and Drug Administration (FDA) regulation called 12CFR11, which involves strict validation of the database and data. Other research may only require standard security and validation. Many AMCs are now using the REDCAP software program to manage data. This national program provides training and can be utilized by researchers directly with some basic training. A major trend in clinical data research takes data from the EMR into a data warehouse to enable Real World Data research. This requires a team to extract data from the EMR, standardize it for research use and work with researchers to extract data for their studies. This team may also include statisticians and data scientists to help analyze the data.

3.3.9 Contract

In addition to the many permanent positions within a health system or hospital, there are usually many contract employees on a short- or long-term basis. This is especially true for a large system implementation, conversion or upgrade, integration of systems from newly acquired hospitals or practices or other major projects, such as moving data to the cloud.

3.4 Knowledge for Job Hunting

In preparing for a career in hospitals and health systems, remember that most people in healthcare are there because it is a mission-driven organization – people are there because they want to be involved in care and healing. Also, be aware of the typical hierarchy, with administrators and physicians at the top and department chairs similar to corporate divisions but with an academic twist since many of the physicians are also faculty in affiliated medical schools. Nurses are essential to the daily work-flow, and a variety of physician extenders, often physician assistants and nurse practitioners, provide much of the prescribing of care. Comfort in working with clinical professionals is essential.

Budget-wise, most of the income is from insurance reimbursement and budgets are usually allocated on an annual basis, sometimes on the academic year rather than calendar year. Based on payer mix (Medicare/Medicaid/private insurance), budgets may be tight if the reimbursement levels are trending down or flat. Most health systems are always looking for efficiencies and some of this has led to the development of innovation centers within the organization. Most now have EMRs as a core IT function, which includes major investment in software and hardware as well as staff to support this 24/7/365 availability. Some hiring processes can be long, involving screening tests and multiple interviews with the hiring manager as well as teams. Job security is usually good in the long term for IT jobs, but can be at risk if the organization decides to outsource major functions.

3.5 Job Description Examples

Here are three examples of job descriptions at health systems to illustrate the type of work one might encounter.

3.5.1 Clinical Informatics Specialist

According to USF, "Clinical informatics specialists are commonly responsible for building and teaching user interfaces to healthcare organization staff, implementing plans to improve patient records management systems, and facilitating communication between the IT team, healthcare providers and other stakeholders" (USF Health Online 2022a). This can mean responsibility for clinical interfaces, cybersecurity, staff training and implementation of new technologies.

3.5.2 Clinical/Business Intelligence Analyst

This job includes database management and queries, usually involving SQL or other tools, integration of various data sources into a data warehouse, development of data visualization and dashboards and data dissemination through reports and dashboards. Also, the role often includes supporting clinical research through management of registries, clinical trial databases and reporting tools. These analysts typically work in teams which may include data scientists (USF Health Online 2022b).

3.5.3 Cybersecurity Analyst

Because healthcare data is increasingly threatened by cyberattacks, this job is essential to healthcare organizations. Job responsibilities include managing firewall security, supporting authentication to health and business data, ensuring that installed or external applications in use have adequate security, management of data access based on roles and ensuring the security of the data center as well as cloud-based applications and databases in use. The role requires teamwork both within the cybersecurity department, the broader IT organization and the health system employees in general. Keeping current on cyber threats and new security technology is essential.

3.6 Job Criteria

3.6.1 Technical Skills

The technical skills within informatics vary by job category. While all need some basic knowledge, like the nature of a relational database and basic data security and privacy, some job categories require a degree in computer science while others necessitate knowledge of a specific system. This can range from a high school diploma with little technical knowledge for a beginner at an IT help desk to a Ph.D. in statistics for a data scientist. For instance, someone developing workflow enhancements in an EMR might need thorough knowledge of that specific EMR, including the majority of the features, while someone supporting the installation and configuration of the EMR would need knowledge of operating systems, the computer language the EMR is running on and the hardware utilized. Programmers who are writing code to insert or extract data from the EMR would need advanced programming skills in the specific language being used. For instance, FHIR typically uses RESTful Web Services. Data analysts supporting the data warehouse would need a thorough understanding of relational databases, query language and tools and data visualization skills. Security analysts would need knowledge of the range of security tools from firewalls to network security including the latest information on how to defeat hacker attacks and policy changes. Informatics training professionals would need knowledge of any system they hope to teach, including some of the technical underpinnings of those systems. Those informaticists who support research would need an understanding of database validation as well as the ability to query EMR and clinical trial data for research analysis.

3.6.2 People Skills

In addition to the technical side, information technology in healthcare requires people skills. Healthcare is a people-centric industry working in teams to improve health. Information technology is no exception. First, even in the most technical role, one is a member of a team. Few projects or products are managed by one person, so team collaboration and communication are key. This includes in-person team meetings, project team meetings and the use of collaboration tools.

Also within an IT department, there are collaboration and project work between teams. Most projects require input at many levels, such as which servers will be required, will the software work on the existing workstations and mobile devices even with different operating systems, what data will be moving between systems, what are the security requirements, etc. It would not be unusual for five or more IT teams to collaborate on any given project. Again, in-person meetings, often led by a project manager, are expected and the use of project management and collaboration tools is essential.

Communication with internal customers is another aspect of people skills required in information technology. While some, like project and product managers or nurse informaticists, might do this more routinely, the ability to understand the needs of clinical and administrative staff is essential. The most important people skill is the ability to translate technical information to clinical staff and clinical and operational needs into technical solutions. While most healthcare professionals have advanced degrees, speaking in very technical terms to explain a solution will turn them off.

Finally, IT professionals need people skills while working on external collaborations. Frequently, IT staff meet with market suppliers to understand how their products may provide solutions to their organizations. Smart negotiating skills with these companies help define requirements and price for the hospital. Collaboration with IT departments in other organizations enables not only learning best practices, but also the success of joint projects in research or use of a common tool, such as at meetings of user groups for applications.

3.6.3 Experience with Healthcare

In most health systems, IT departments prefer to hire someone with healthcare experience. Part of the reason is that some IT systems are specifically designed for healthcare. The most obvious example is the Electronic Medical Record, which is now considered the core of what informatics supports. Understanding medical technology is a requirement in almost every IT job within a hospital or health system. Even knowing how medicine is divided into specialties and what nurses do on a day-to-day basis is essential. Then there is the 24/7 nature of healthcare, which requires IT professionals to be on-call for emergencies. Healthcare as a highly regulated industry requires that even IT professionals know HIPAA, reporting requirements and hospital policies at a minimum. Healthcare is also different from other industries in that its focus is providing care for the sick. With a more mission-driven approach, healthcare organizations want employees who are dedicated to the mission. Some even consider all employees, including those in IT, as "caregivers." One former CIO said he preferred to hire nurses particularly for supporting the EMR and workflow, not just because of the familiarity

Recommended Skills

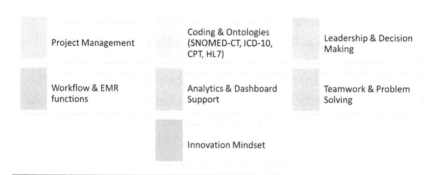

Figure 3.1 Skills Recommended For Informatics Work in Hospitals & Health Systems.

with day-to-day clinical care but also because of their commitment to a mission-driven organization.

For those coming to hospitals or health systems from outside of healthcare, there are options for internships or even volunteering. Some have taken the route of working for a healthcare startup before moving into one of these positions. Becoming familiar with medical terminology and health technology can also help. Some come to the field with personal or family experience with healthcare and the motivation to improve it.

3.7 International

Many large health systems recruit international healthcare professionals. They are usually familiar with hiring those on work visas and H-1B visas specifically for information technology professionals. These employers will look at both technical proficiency and language proficiency in the hiring process.

3.8 Keywords for Job Search

As you search for career opportunities in hospitals and health systems, there are some recommended keywords and phrases to get you started. Suggestions include:

■ Hospital IT, healthcare information technology, health/ medical informatics, healthcare analytics, EMR/EHR analyst, healthcare cybersecurity, digital health, remote patient monitoring.

3.9 Summary

Hospitals and health systems provide a multitude of job roles for the IT professional. The field has certainly experienced growth and is projected to continue. For example, the need for a host of informatics professionals includes everything from application support to cybersecurity to analytics. Project and product management are areas of growth in many health systems as new products and applications are evaluated and rolled out.

In addition to the standard job categories described here, new ones continue to emerge. As more cloud-based applications are developed and new systems to engage patients expand, job roles and opportunities will expand with them. Remote monitoring and telehealth – where patients are monitored or provided care through voice or video technology – will continue to expand with a need to manage patient-generated health data and video visits. Telehealth centers are becoming common both for patient-facing interactions as well as provider-to-provider telemedicine consults, such as teleICU and radiology (Marr 2022; Mass Challenge 2022).

References

"Clinical Informatics Specialist: Job Description and Guide." *USF Health Online*, December 2, 2022a. www.usfhealthonline.com/resources/health-informatics/clinical-informatics-specialist/.

"Future of Healthcare Report: Exploring Healthcare Stakeholders' Expectations for the Next Chapter." *HIMSS*, September 20, 2022. www.himss.org/resources/future-healthcare-report-exploring-healthcare-stakeholders-expectations-next-chapter.

"Healthcare Data Scientist Job Description and Salary Information." *USF Health Online*, December 2, 2022b. www.usfhealthonline.com/resources/health-informatics/healthcare-data-scientist-job-description/.

Marr, Bernard. "The Five Biggest Healthcare Tech Trends in 2022." *Forbes Magazine,* January 10, 2022. www.forbes.com/sites/bernardmarr/2022/01/10/the-five-biggest-healthcare-tech-trends-in-2022/?sh=ce6c4b454d01.

"Rising Trends in Digital Health: 5 Technologies That Will Define the Future of Healthcare." *Mass Challenge,* May 25, 2022. https://masschallenge.org/articles/digital-health-trends/.

Chapter 4

Careers in Health Information Technology (Health IT) Companies

"Every healthcare system or industry group is different. But if you have the basic fundamentals, you can apply them anywhere. If you have database knowledge, knowledge of SQL, or statistical programming knowledge (R and Python, even standard packages that involve those), that alone can get you very far in this industry. Just having the interest and drive to learn a new domain often is enough."

– Dr. Jason Gilder
Informatics Scientific Subject Matter Expert, federal contractor supporting HHS ASPR BARDA Division of Research Innovation and Ventures (DRIVe)

DOI: 10.4324/9781003185727-4

4.1 Introduction to Health Information Technology Companies

This chapter describes the many opportunities for health informatics careers in the private sector, focusing on products and services in health information technology (health IT) and consumer health. This category is rather broad and includes startups (e.g., biotechnology, genomic startups), health IT companies (e.g., electronic health record/EHR software, medical equipment, etc.), innovation arms of companies (innovation labs of companies or health IT companies) and consumer health companies (e.g., divisions of information technology companies, wellness, pharmaceutical companies, etc.).

The ecosystem of digital health would not be as effective without vendor partners or health IT companies. Health information companies are making life-changing advancements in digital health to augment and improve scientific insights, improve patient health and reduce clinician burden to deliver the best value to their customers. To help achieve this progress, there are many career opportunities for job applicants trained in health informatics. These jobs could be located at the company offices (hybrid or remote), or they could be co-located at a client site. For example, EHR companies' hospital clients may have employees located onsite at the hospital so that they can be readily available for hands-on system work or client involvement. You may be asked to be onsite with a client part of the time or for the duration of a weeks- or months-long project.

Aligned with the digital transformation of healthcare, there are a growing number of job opportunities related to health information technology. Health information companies need skilled technology workers to manage existing systems, implement new systems, integrate peripheral data sources and devices, design new interfaces, innovate and then manage those innovations. Technology recruiters for healthcare CPSI and Robert Half report that there are more opportunities for tech professionals looking to enter or advance their career by transitioning to healthcare IT (Pratt 2022). Moreover, Emsi Burning Glass (now Lightcast), a specialist in labor market analytics, shows 122% growth of data engineer positions, 108% growth of data scientist positions and 107% growth of web designer jobs from 2019 to 2022 in this industry (Pratt 2022).

Readers will see examples of companies at the time of this writing. Know that the company names may change, as they are merged with or acquired by other companies or exit the market. Change happens rapidly across the health IT industry, so please keep this in mind.

4.2 A Word About Health Informatics in Big Tech

Another relatively new phenomenon is the growth of healthcare teams in big tech companies. These include jobs in cloud services, wearable technology, data analytics, digital health apps and more. For instance, Google (Alphabet) has expanded its healthcare division, first by the development of Verily initially in life sciences, then with the acquisition of Fitbit and the use of Google Cloud for healthcare data. Apple has hired physicians and technologists to expand the Apple Health App to connect to EMR and wellness data, and the use of the Apple watch not just for fitness but also for medical issues like atrial fibrillation. Microsoft is also using its cloud service and analytics in Azure. Meta is investing in virtual reality, both as a service to consumers and to healthcare professionals for collaboration and training. One big tech company which previously only serviced life sciences, Oracle, is the first of this group to actually purchase an EMR, Cerner. Oracle's cloud services will have a big impact in the future of this endeavor.

4.3 A Day in the Life

A typical day in the life of a health informaticist for a health information technology company can vary widely as there are many roles a person with this skill set can occupy. Moreover, there are many types of health IT companies, from large software companies to small startups. For example, a data analyst for an electronic health record (EHR) company may be charged with creating analysis plans, gathering and preparing the correct data, running analysis using R, Excel or SPSS and then creating a report to share findings with the broad group of stakeholders, both internal (other health IT co-workers) or external (clients at hospital systems).

Data scientist, Dr. Jason Gilder has worked in innovation labs and health IT startups and is now an Informatics Scientific Subject Matter Expert federal contractor supporting HHS ASPR BARDA Division of Research Innovation and Ventures (DRIVe). Dr. Gilder spoke with us about a day in the life of an informaticist working with an innovation lab. In describing a typical day, he mentioned that those working in data and data management may be involved in a variety of activities. Specifically, they might help to build and work with the core platform, specify or conduct data analytics, identify eligible members for pilot programs or collect data once members are enrolled. It is also common for others in roles related to data to work with patients' reported outcomes, surveys and questionnaires. That is, a health informaticist on the team may be in charge of which questions need to be asked in a survey or questionnaire for any number of projects. For example, they may evaluate and analyze data to find out which patient programs are working well, which ones need tweaking or modification or whether results may inform population health initiatives for the organization, like increasing the rate of vaccinations for children or decreasing incidence of smoking. Other projects may be focused on identifying best practices for preventive care, managing health and illness at home, reducing costs and improving quality.

4.4 What Skill Sets Do Job Candidates Need?

There are many job roles in health IT organizations in which most of the learning and growth come with actual work experience. Dr. Gilder stated that typically, a person should come to the job with at least a bachelor's degree, and a willingness to learn new skills and domain knowledge. A candidate could improve their opportunities through having healthcare experience, but it is not necessary. Moreover, the candidate could also enhance opportunities by having a set of technical skills that are helpful for the job (e.g., R, Python, SQL, etc.). He says: "Anything on cloud infrastructures is important. If candidates are interested in programming software, Java is still the primary language to know and use. In more scientific programming or ad-hoc programming, R and Python are the big ones. Jupyter Notebook environment is still heavily used." Whichever company you work for may have its own training courses and you can get certifications as well. Of course, technologies and trends change quickly, so the technology you will need to know will change. Dr. Gilder mentioned that skills in these technologies will get you far in the industry, but **it is important to demonstrate that you have an interest and drive to keep learning something new**.

Dr. Gilder shared an example of someone he knew in a similar business who started with a bachelor's degree in mathematics and was eager to learn. This person worked with a team to go into EMR systems, billing systems, claim systems and bring the data into the cloud so that it could be standard-ized, normalized and made into a common format. That is, the task was to take different types of data from different databases, and organize it in a similar way across all records and fields, so that it could be analyzed and some sense could be made of it. This person then went on to become a leader at a major health information company, and later a senior vice president at a leading health IT consulting firm. The differenti-ators included that the person demonstrated **willingness and capability to learn, was trainable, picked up new skills and was adaptable**.

It is important to have core capabilities like problem solv-ing, problem identification, being able to break complex problems into small chunks, and the ability to manage that in a good way and then to work with colleagues and teammates on solving the problem. To accomplish this, **communica-tion is central to the informaticist's job**. Depending on the role, there is a huge need for being a kind of "translator" or "glue," connecting clinical roles to technology needs. For instance, this can mean speaking with clinicians, speaking with researchers and understanding their questions, needs and what they are trying to do, then translating that into techni-cal requirements that engineers and developers can actually understand. Without the intermediary, there will be miscom-munication. You have to listen and ask questions in order to learn about what is needed.

4.5 What is an Example of a Typical Data Analysis?

Dr. Gilder shared an example of the type of data analysis needed for a study. He mentioned that you may need to iden-tify cases in the (de-identified) database of people of a certain age range who have diabetes. Then you will need to clarify those with type 2 diabetes, then clarify those with type 2 diabetes who are currently being treated. Typically, you have to have informed discussions with stakeholders to understand what is actually needed for the data analysis, as there may be many relevant data fields. It is important to verify the end goal with the researcher, stakeholders and clinicians.

4.6 What Job Roles Will a Health Informatics Specialist Have?

In this field, you have an opportunity to play a big part in shaping the strategy, requirements and plan for a product. There is a significant need for project management, program management and product management. Requirements gathering, understanding the true needs of the people using or who are affected by the product (stakeholders) and being the "translator" between clinical and technology specialists is highly sought-after. Some jobs may involve some coding or programming, but not all of them do. It is a good idea to be aware of the needs of stakeholders and what is being asked of the innovation team or the health IT organization.

4.7 Do I Need Certifications for These Jobs?

Dr. Gilder noted that job seekers may distinguish themselves with earned certifications, but these can be viewed as an extra or an added bonus. Certifications may be helpful for people who've been out of school for a while. It shows that they are interested, they are capable of learning and they are capable of picking up different skills. He says, "It's not a requirement, but it's a starting point." For example, certifications may include CPHIMS (certified professional in healthcare information and management systems); CAHIMS (certified associate in healthcare information and management systems); RHIT (registered health information technologist); RHIA (registered health information administrator); or AHIC (AMIA health informatics certification). Any number of Epic certifications are desirable, but individuals are not eligible on their own; instead, these certifications need to be achieved through sponsorship by a hospital system.

Dr. Gilder reminds job seekers that they do not need to meet every requirement listed in a job advertisement. It is important to demonstrate how your skills address the needs of the listed role, how you have demonstrated your skills in past experiences and that you are teachable and can learn new techniques and skills. While many skills can be picked up on the job, it will be helpful to a potential employee in this arena to get up to speed on the latest open-source technologies like FHIR standards or open-source tools (e.g., OpenEMPI to assist with patient matching to reduce duplicate patient records).

4.8 What is a Typical Day in the Life of a Data Analyst?

When asked about a typical day in the life of a data analyst in a health IT company, Dr. Gilder mentioned that the data analyst usually has to process a lot of data from multiple sources. He describes an example that they might be looking in an EMR system to find out the workflow, where the information is stored and how things are presented or coded. Then they have to figure out how to translate that into a common format. There is usually a data standard, or a data common model that the organization is using. So they have to perform mapping or translation. The analyst may then have to go in to find out how data was captured and figure out how to translate it, re-coding if necessary. This is a big piece of problem solving for data analysts. He continues, that often they have separate groups working on that translation or semantic normalization. They'll sample all the codes and build a crosswalk, or a translation map. There are semi-automated tools involved to do this, including machine learning models or code libraries. As an example, OpenRefine is an open-source tool for cleaning data and transforming it from one format to another. Other tools include Weka, KNIME and CLAMP (clinical language annotation, modeling and processing toolkit). MetaMap is a tool that maps free text to the Unified Medical Language System (UMLS), a set of files and software that enables interoperability by bringing together many health and biomedical vocabularies and standards (www.nlm.nih.gov/research/umls/index.html). Possible uses for this kind of data transformation include linking terms and codes among the hospital, pharmacy and insurance company or coordinating care among several departments within a hospital.

4.9 Informatics Roles

4.9.1 Health IT Companies/EHR Vendors

Health IT companies like EHR vendors (e.g., Cerner, Epic, Meditech, etc.) have a number of career opportunities for those with informatics preparation. For example, there are roles centered on product development, product implementation, product use, maintenance and optimization. Product development roles include product owner, product manager, business analyst, information systems manager and data architect. The other roles (implementation, use, maintenance and optimization) may be co-located with clients, or at least might require travel to clients and periods of time working with clients onsite to ensure that the health IT company product is successfully integrated and functioning as designed. In terms of maintenance and optimization, companies will need skilled people to process any issues contributing to errors. These liaisons may work with end-users at the hospital or healthcare center to report issues, make updates/patches to software and communicate back to the stakeholder groups or people working on the administration, clinical and technical teams.

4.9.2 Innovation Labs

Innovation labs exist across the spectrum of health IT and health information-related fields. They are places where cross-functional teams can work together to come up with new ideas for solutions or products for the company. These products can be for both external (paying customers) and internal stakeholders (co-workers). For example, perhaps the innovation lab is developing, iterating and testing a new mobile application for customers. Moreover, the lab could be designing and testing a new artificial intelligence (AI) algorithm to help their own co-workers review detailed material more efficiently. Typically, the innovation team works to develop a minimum viable product (MVP) or prototype for the business to demonstrate how it works. Then, the business can decide to expand the product or try something else. Innovation labs, in general, are places where co-workers can test out ideas for new business products.

4.9.3 Consumer Health/Pharmacy/ Medical Technology

Consumer health and pharmacy companies (e.g., CVS, Walgreens, Walmart, etc.) are all developing health information components to manage patient health or engage in the supply chain in global markets. These organizations are now engaged in looking for health informatics specialists to maintain databases, run reports, inform best practices, etc. These organizations may partner with other companies for their expertise here (e.g., Microsoft's health and supply chain division). Have you gotten a flu shot or other vaccine at a pharmacy lately? Maybe you scheduled your appointment via the website or app or you checked in and completed forms electronically before you got your shot. Those electronic systems were made possible by the work of health IT professionals.

Medical technology companies (e.g., Baxter Healthcare) may have jobs listed in information technology. For example, Baxter Healthcare lists a job description for "senior project manager of technology & innovation." The job description indicates that they are looking for a candidate who could have a degree in informatics; skills and experience they seek are consistent with other health informatics jobs.

4.9.4 *Startups in Biotechnology and Digital Health*

Startup enterprises in digital health, health information technology and biotechnology are growing as the field engages in digital transformation. These types of companies exist as larger well-established corporations; however, the smaller startup enterprises typically are building, researching and promoting only a few product lines in digital health. For example, these companies may be developing new digital tools for patients to monitor health at home through biosensors or more specific use of the smartphone camera, artificial intelligence tools for pharmaceutical development, mobile apps for health management in monitoring heart rhythms or tools to make it more efficient for clinicians to access electronic health records and diagnostic images remotely. Job seekers who are interested in these types of unique and growing companies might find them accessible in organizations like business or specific digital health business incubators, "tech hub" or "innovation corridor" programs by state, county and NGO groups. Spinoffs and startups can also be sponsored by larger for-profit entities (e.g., Google, Apple, etc.).

4.10 Knowledge for Job Hunting

As you consider a job in a health information technology (health IT) company or a "vendor," as hospitals and clinicians often refer to them, remember that typically these organizations are for-profit, and sometimes publicly-traded companies. People working there typically want to make a difference by improving health or healthcare through their products. Pay attention to the goals of the company and decide whether you are interested in and motivated to help achieve those goals in healthcare, as many companies focus on eliminating or reducing disease, increasing independence of patients, improving health outcomes and improving quality of care. As employees work toward achieving the goals for the company, they are charged with making their products and services profitable. As a result, company initiatives will be mindful of cost and return on investment. As you engage with clients, you will be asked to mitigate risks and issues; you typically will need to review potential changes or updates to the product with many different stakeholders to evaluate the impact of that change for the client, your own production team, the sales team, as well as those in the company who provide support services for clients. Your work will need to be documented and available for knowledge sharing among many co-workers. If anyone in the company is the sole keeper of too much information, that is a risk to the health and success of the company. Plan on communicating with leadership and team members often so that there is a team approach to addressing client concerns or developing new products. Be aware of the organizational chart of your company, knowing that the executives (e.g., chief executive officer, board of directors, etc.) ultimately steer decision making in the company in close alignment with senior management and leadership. Health IT companies, like many corporations, have organizational charts that show to whom you report and your process for work activities.

This vendor community of health IT companies, whether they are software groups, innovation labs or medical device manufacturers, are an essential part of the digital health environment and use informed, quality information technology to improve health and healthcare. They typically deliver these solutions quickly, benefiting both their bottom line and the quality of care offered to patients by clinicians. In many cases, health IT vendors are actively involved in partnering with hospitals, clinicians, pharmacists and researchers to advance quality of care. You can see this through many health IT vendor sponsorships of academic and clinician meetings and organizations (e.g., HIMSS, AMIA, etc.); service on working groups for standards organizations (e.g., HL7). Moreover, many health IT vendors have organizations, like the HIMSS Electronic Health Record Association (EHRA), whose focus is on collaborative efforts to accelerate health IT adoption, assist member companies with regulatory compliance, advance interoperable systems and improve quality and efficiency of patient care through the use of technology (www.linkedin.com/company/ehrassociation/).

Like any organization, a health IT company will adjust career opportunities relative to the economic market. With this in mind, not all opportunities in health IT vendor companies will be a typical full-time employee or "FTE." Instead, there may be shorter-term or project-based opportunities to work with them as a contractor, with both an option to renew the contract or an option to join the company officially. Of course, there are tradeoffs in this type of role, as there are typically no financial bonus, health benefits, or paid vacation or sick time. However, a role as a contractor may allow you to demonstrate that your skill set transfers to the company, giving you experience and opening opportunities for more permanent positions. The takeaway here is that it is important to know that both short- and long-term plans are necessary for career planning. You may be able to be more flexible at different times. You can have success and gain experience with a health IT company without a traditional full-time job role.

4.11 Job Description Examples

A few common health informatics jobs in health information companies include (but are not limited to): business analyst, health IT liaison, EHR liaison, product owner, project manager, data warehouse manager, database manager, data analyst, health information technology, health IT, EHR informatics, innovation health IT, consumer health specialist, health supply chain specialist, integration specialist, implementation manager, data migration specialist, etc. We describe a few of these jobs in detail here.

4.11.1 *Project Manager*

A project manager for a health IT company is generally tasked with overseeing a project from start to finish. A person in this role will work with a product manager or product owner, the development manager and team, as well as the quality assurance team members for the project. A person in this role typically communicates with stakeholders in the business and on the team about the scope, timeline and cost of the project. Overall, the project manager's job is to facilitate the project meeting quality standards and the requirements of the business and that it is on time and within the budget. Many people set themselves apart in this role by having a Project Management Professional (PMP) designation, but it is not necessarily required. There are various levels of the role of project manager, from assistant to senior to director of project management.

4.11.2 Clinical Informatics Specialist or Senior Team Lead in Health Informatics

Responsibilities might include providing informatics guidance and acting as a liaison between the health system department(s) and IT to provide solutions by leveraging operational, business and clinical experience and informatics knowledge. Even though the job is through a health IT company, this job may be co-located onsite at the client hospital or medical center. The clinical informatics specialist may need to be someone with clinical expertise or experience (e.g., nurse). The team lead role in health informatics generally does not require someone to be a clinician.

4.11.3 Health Informatics/Medical Informatics Consultant

This person is asked to serve as a resource and liaison in the development, implementation, and support of health information technology utilized by medical staff. Organizes and evaluates incoming issues and requests and determines prioritization and mitigation plans, and contributes to decisions about whether something needs to be escalated. Conducts testing and maintenance of applications and related technology. Develops and facilitates provider education to ensure competency related to all aspects of hardware and software. Works collaboratively across stakeholder groups including medical staff, administration and IT to identify and implement new and/or enhanced technology and process solutions. The applicant for this position may or may not need to be a clinician.

4.11.4 *Product Owner/Product Manager*

A product owner and product manager are both part of the product team and meet with end-users and clients to understand the requirements and needs for the product (e.g. module of an EHR; upgrade of an existing telehealth software). The product manager is responsible for strategy and a roadmap for the product, working closely with the product owner who ensures that the product meets and exceeds the expectations and requirements of the user or client. Both of these roles work and communicate across the product team to ensure that the right level of functionality and quality are delivered in a given time frame and on budget. They make decisions about how to proceed if there are challenges to the time frame or budget and manage the backlog if items need to be moved.

4.11.5 *Database Manager*

Responsibilities typically include the development and implementation of the SQL server life cycle as it relates to application needs, as well as working directly with peers, vendors and application developers to create database strategies that support the application and operational needs of customers, including meeting all regulatory, security, privacy and accessibility requirements. You may also be responsible for performing database system management functions (e.g., software installs, version upgrades and configuration management, security), designing, implementing, and managing complex database environments and defining database objects and relationships as indicated based on requirements of the application. You may also handle ensuring that database environments are properly installed and implemented and utilize appropriate backup strategies. You may be partnering with the Project Management Office to participate in all phases of project implementation. You'll utilize and maintain appropriate change control procedures and standards. Typically, the applicant for this position does not need to be a clinician.

4.12 Job Criteria

4.12.1 Technical Skills

Technology skills (across all sectors) continue to be in demand in healthcare, with an emphasis on health informatics and data science. These skills can be in a variety of areas, but some of the most sought-after include software development, programming, data analysis (including predictive analytics), data science, data visualization, database management, machine learning, artificial intelligence, cybersecurity, robotic process automation and extended reality (augmented reality, virtual reality and mixed reality). Other skill sets include project management, change management and administrative abilities.

Some of these jobs (e.g., clinical integration consultant, project manager of innovation and technology, product owner or business analyst) involve the product development, management and support of health information-related products, and so it is important to understand the evergreen principles of health informatics and the required integrations with other health systems. For example, new programming languages may become the standard, but knowing one makes it easier to learn a second. Other roles at these companies (e.g., product specialist, sales representative) require a familiarity with information technology and health informatics principles, because you may be interfacing with clinicians and informaticians in healthcare systems and other clients, so you would need to understand the value of the product and how it would help to solve pain points. For example, you would need to know about and communicate how your health IT product (e.g., EHR) would help clinicians, how it would save them time or show documentation clearly to interested stakeholders (e.g., pharmacy, nurses, patient, other clinicians, etc.). Knowledge of clinical workflow and informatics patterns are also important as the products (e.g., EHR or medical equipment) are maintained and supported over time.

Technical expertise in data, analytics, security and beyond are sought. In a parallel manner, job candidates with domain-specific knowledge in a variety of related areas will be desired. This can include not only clinical and technical areas of expertise, but also communication, relationship building and problem solving. There are many opportunities for you to help technology companies connect with potential customers and maintain accounts over the years. Your communication, customer service and research skills are needed in helping to understand pain points among your clients and finding new ways to add value. You may find yourself organizing innovation opportunities and brainstorming sessions among your colleagues about this.

Recommended Skills

Keeping organized/ Project Management	Good Communication Skills: Verbal & Written	Leadership & Decision Making
Understanding Client Needs	Analytics with SQL, Excel, R, or Python	Teamwork & Problem Solving
Managing data and generating reports	Integrative Standards (FHIR, HL7, RESTful API)	Awareness of Policies & Regulations

Figure 4.1 Skills Recommended For Informatics Work in Health Information Technology Companies.

4.12.2 People Skills

People skills or soft skills in demand include good communication (verbal and written), time management, collaboration with a team, and leadership. These are critical skills in any thriving business or organization. Soft skills are necessary for job roles in health informatics because of the many opportunities employees have to act as a liaison between technical specialists and clinical clients. A person in these roles needs to be a savvy and thoughtful communicator. In other words, this person needs to feel comfortable enough in learning about highly specified clinical workflow and rationale, balanced with understanding technical specifics of what is possible for the development team to produce based on the technological platform and interoperability capability of the health IT. This means that the soft skills of the well-adjusted worker include the capability to say "no, I don't understand . . . would you explain that to me?" This acknowledgement of not knowing something but wanting to learn to better solve the client's problem, is essential. It shows confidence in your capabilities and strong self-esteem to admit vulnerability and say you don't know but take active steps to learn quickly.

Jobs in these kinds of organizations tend to be team-oriented instead of siloed individual work. The co-workers on your team will work with you to deliver value to clients in healthcare. One of the advantages of working in health information companies is the wide variety of specialized backgrounds of your co-workers and colleagues. Your colleagues may come from a wide variety of specialized backgrounds, including product and finance specialists, clinicians, user experience researchers and designers, health science researchers, engineers or developers, project managers, informaticists, salespeople, consultants and technical support specialists. This variety in roles and areas of expertise supports problem solving in the digital health information ecosystem. In other words, this career subset is one where you want to have or be willing to develop good interpersonal skills for co-worker relationship development. As we read in the introduction chapter, job candidates are more likely to succeed if they demonstrate their abilities to solve problems both as an individual and as part of a group.

4.12.3 Experience with Healthcare

Clinical experience can be helpful to provide context and experience on how health IT products and services are positioned. Still, it is not imperative that employees have clinical experience. It really depends on the role. In most cases, people who demonstrate an ability to learn quickly and to have a good attitude about working with a team, but who may not have clinical experience, are welcomed into many roles in a health IT organization.

4.13 International

Many large health IT companies recruit international healthcare professionals. They are usually familiar with hiring those on work visas and H-1B visas specifically for information technology professionals. These employers will look at both technical proficiency and language proficiency in the hiring process.

4.14 Keywords for Job Search

As you search for career opportunities in health information companies, there are some recommended keywords and phrases to search. Suggestions include:

- health data analysis, health data management, health IT, innovation in health data, innovation in health information, health startups, healthcare supply chain, health information products, health database, health data analytics, consumer health informatics

4.15 Summary

The electronic health record (EHR) was the key technology used in moving paper-based records to digital records. Since 2010, when the HITECH Act provided financial incentives for eligible hospitals and providers to implement and meaningfully use the EHR, the majority (96%) of hospitals have adopted the EHR (ONC 2022). As the field of health informatics looks forward into best practice models for healthcare into the next several decades, digital transformation is essential to move to the next phase, where clinicians and patients can leverage digital healthcare tools to improve quality of care.

The next few decades will use the EHR as a basis on which to grow. This includes the use of secure, accurate data and cloud platforms through which healthcare organizations and health information companies can implement and optimize information systems, share data and utilize it for predictive analytics and improving the quality of care (i.e., evaluating social determinants of health to offer support to geographical regions that are most negatively affected or in need of support). This intersection of health technology, information and people forms the basis for digital transformation. Career opportunities in this space will continue to grow, led by healthcare professionals and health information specialists. Employers will be looking for qualified candidates who have technical and communication skills, domain expertise and can complete a project either individually or in a group. Employers will need candidates who understand digital transformation and its impact on health and the healthcare ecosystem.

References

Committee on Energy and Commerce. "Implementation of the Health Information Technology for Economic and Clinical Health (HITECH) Act: Hearing Before the Subcommittee on Health of the Committee on Energy and Commerce, House of Representatives, One Hundred Eleventh Congress, Second Session §." July 27, 2010.

"Electronic Health Record Association | Linkedin." Accessed January 16, 2023. www.linkedin.com/company/ehrassociation.

Office of the National Coordinator (ONC) for Health Information Technology. "Adoption of Electronic Health Records by Hospital Service Type 2019–2021." *Health IT Quick Stat #60*, April 2022. https://www.healthit.gov/data/quickstats/adoption-electronic-health-records-hospital-service-type-2019-2021.

Pratt, Mark. "How to Get a Job in Healthcare IT." *Computerworld*, June 16, 2022. https://www-computerworld-com.cdn.ampproject.org/c/s/www.computerworld.com/article/3663674/how-to-get-a-job-in-healthcare-it.amp.html.

Chapter 5

Careers in Health Insurance/Payer Organizations

"From a high level, informaticians in a payer organization use information to make members' or patients' health care better in terms of both their experience and outcomes."

–Mr. Devendra Rao
Executive Director, Information Technology at BlueCross BlueShield Association

5.1 Introduction to Health Insurance and Health Insurance Informatics

Payers are a critical part of the healthcare system in the United States, and health informaticians have expanding job opportunities in these organizations. What's a payer? Payers are responsible for enrolling patients, determining eligibility, processing

DOI: 10.4324/9781003185727-5

claims and paying medical professionals for providing care. Healthcare payers include both health insurance companies and public care agencies like Medicare and Medicaid. These types of organizations are not providers, but instead they set service rates, collect payments, process claims and pay provider claims (www.collectivemedical.com, accessed October 2022).

Let's review a bit of background about payers for health insurance companies and how they are an active stakeholder in the healthcare landscape. Healthcare is provided to patients by clinicians with pre-arrangements for payment from payers including health insurance companies and government agencies (e.g., Center for Medicare and Medicaid Services or CMS). An efficient and effective payer system allows healthcare providers to have the resources they need to offer reliable and quality services to their patients. Both providers and payers rely on data to inform their tasks, processing and decision making. Health informatics specialists who can work with healthcare data offer tremendous value to insurance companies and other payers.

Examples of payers:

■ Health insurance companies are the most common type of payer in the United States. As of 2020, 64.3% of Americans under age 65 were covered by private health insurance, either through their employer (56.6%) or by direct purchase (6.7%) (U.S. Census 2020). Payment structures in this space are usually organized into the following categories:
  – HMO: Health Maintenance Organization is typically advantageous to those who wish to spend less money on deductibles and shared costs (e.g., copays). However, people enrolled in an HMO will only be reimbursed for care provided by a predetermined network of providers. There is typically limited flexibility on how and where care is provided.
  – PPO: Preferred Provider Organizations offers more flexibility in choice of clinician, allowing some

reimbursement from providers within or outside of the network of providers. These plans tend to cost more money out of pocket for patients, both through premiums, deductibles and shared costs. However, these plans tend to provide more choices for the patient.

■ Government agencies, including the state and federal programs through the Center for Medicare and Medicaid Services (CMS):

- Over 65 million people are enrolled in Medicare, as of March 2023 (including both fee for service and Medicare Advantage plans) (CMS.gov 2023). "Medicare is a federal health insurance program paying for covered healthcare services for most people aged 65 and older and for certain permanently disabled individuals under age 65." (U.S. Health Care Coverage and Spending, February 2023, Congressional Research Service, https://sgp.fas.org/crs/misc/IF10830.pdf).

- There are 91.3 million enrollees on Medicaid, including 84.3 million on Medicaid and 7 million on Children's Health Insurance Program (CHIP) (CMS.gov 2023). Medicaid, funded through both federal and state funds, is the largest source of funding for medical and health-related services for people with low income in the United States.

■ ACO: Accountable Care Organizations (ACOs) are groups of doctors, hospitals and other healthcare providers who come together voluntarily to give coordinated high-quality care to the Medicare patients they serve (www.cms.gov/Medicare/Medicare-Fee-for- Service-Payment/ACO). These provider/payer arrangements help to coordinate care for patients so that they get the care they need in an efficient way, especially those managing chronic illness or multiple comorbidities This coordinated care effort aims to deliver the right care, prevent medical errors and remove duplicate testing, thereby reducing costs.

5.2 How Health Informatics Specialists Work in Payer Organizations

Payers are aligned with healthcare organizations, providers and hospital systems to facilitate reimbursement for healthcare services and care provided. In order to accomplish this, they utilize billing and coding processes for care. As a result, it is important for payer organizations to have skilled employees who understand medical coding, interoperability mechanisms (e.g., FHIR), data sharing standards (e.g., HL7), analysis and reporting of data and how to work with health data in a private and secure manner. For example, an analyst working for the health insurance company may need to upload data from two different electronic health record systems: one from the primary care office and another from an emergency department of a hospital using a different EHR. It is vital to be able to identify those different sources and related codes and upload the pertinent information into the patient's payer record. Beyond the technical and procedural knowledge, it is important to have employees who can communicate with their teammates and customers in a professional manner. Health informatics is an excellent preparation for work in these domains.

Payers operate beyond a reactive model of solely processing and paying for patient care. They are actively engaged in strategies for how to keep their clients/patients healthy and doing a better job of managing their health. For example, many of the larger payer organizations, like United Healthcare, have individual member wellness programs (www.uhc.com/health-and-wellness) to encourage clients to learn about health and wellness to improve their own health or that of a loved one. This kind of program allows clients the opportunity to learn more about certain diseases (e.g., cancer or diabetes) and the risk factors or symptoms to which they should be paying attention. Other payer organizations leverage the vast amount of data they have to analyze and report on lessons learned about wellness among clients. For example, Blue Cross Blue Shield (www.bcbs.com/the-health-of-america/topics/wellness#topic-reports) creates "data driven insights to improve the health of all Americans" by offering reports on issues impacting health and wellness. To support these initiatives, payers employ predictive analytics and other models of analyzing data from clients to inform better decision making. This model expands the need for informatics professionals in their organizations to manage data, run predictive analytics and share insights with company leaders based on their analysis. These roles exist in the traditional payer organization format, or they may exist in spin-off organizations or divisions of the primary group. Helping people manage their health reduces future potential care costs and thus claims for the payer.

Payers are complex organizations, and may have a number of subsidiaries or spin-off divisions focused on research or innovation. For example, there are a number of payers who have spin-off divisions for data management and analysis (e.g., Optum Labs as part of UnitedHealthCare; or one of the innovation divisions of Blue Cross Blue Shield or Kaiser Permanente). Beyond new divisions, payers are also investing in health IT companies as they align to their strategic goals. For example, Highmark and Guidewell invested (Raths 2022) in a kidney disease population management company called Healthmap, built to detect kidney disease early, and recommend clinically proven interventions to delay or slow disease progression.

5.3 Informatics Roles

Informatics roles in payer organizations are similar to other stakeholder groups, especially those related to database management, predictive analytics, mobile apps and reporting. As a result, payer or insurance organizations employ informatics professionals in roles such as clinical informaticist, business analysts, health informatics specialist and database administrators. These roles involve familiarity with and use of databases, communication with interdisciplinary team members to identify the best way to analyze and report findings (e.g., dashboards). In the government payer programs (e.g., Medicare, Medicaid, CHIP) informaticists may also work with team members to develop models and metrics to inform policy decision making or monitor newly contracted managed care plans. These government payer roles exist on the national, state and local levels, so it is important to review all of these areas.

Payer organizations also employ leadership roles in informatics, including senior management roles as a medical informatics analyst, director of clinical informatics and chief information officer. These roles may focus on digital transformation of systems in the organization. They may also focus on the usability of information systems, identifying opportunities for clinical process improvements and leading optimization efforts. Leaders in informatics roles work interactively with people in the organization, evaluating processes and technology to ensure they are aligned to strategic goals. Informatics roles align to initiatives in which the payer uses data to inform decision making and strategy to improve clinical outcomes and efficiencies.

Database-related jobs in payer organizations can also include tasks like conducting claims research or verifying member history, provider outreach and confirming medical record requests. Other related database jobs may be those utilized in reporting to CMS and other government quality measure checks. Employees would be expected to maintain HIPAA standards and confidentiality of protected health information.

Payers take large amounts of data and feed it into different data warehouses, where it is processed, cleaned and batched into episodes of care across many different providers.

Throughout this process, informaticians may be using algorithms to remove duplicate records. In pre-processing, informaticians or analysts may be examining correlations between clinical procedure, type of medication or rehabilitation used and outcomes. For example, analysts may be looking at the efficacy of new pharmaceutical therapies or new drugs. Analysts may be called upon to examine health conditions in certain zip codes in order to identify ways to improve health. Data analysis in payer organizations may also include the risk associated groups of members at new clients or companies looking to offer health insurance to its employees. These calculations to determine how much money they need to pay in premium may look at family histories and risk factors. Most aggregate analysis is done using de-identified data.

5.4 Day in the Life: Business Analyst

Jessica Pollack is a business analyst with a major Midwest health insurance company. Her typical daily activities include taking requests from other departments for reports or dashboards and gathering the specifications so they can be handed along to programmers. To gather specifications, she does some research/prep work based on what was shared in the request and then hosts a meeting with the requesters to go through it. They discuss their workflow processes and documentation steps, where data is captured, context for why they need reporting, what they want to see in the output or visuals, etc. She produces a formal document with the details, and it gets appropriately prioritized and passed to a programmer. Then she helps to manage the project as it moves through to the point of release to production.

When asked about what she enjoys most about her work, she mentioned that her work allows a lot of learning and cross-training. Not only does she have her primary role as a business analyst, but she also helps with quality checking some of the reports when they're ready or even doing some of the programming.

When asked about what the future state of health informatics work looks like for payer organizations, Ms. Pollack reminds us that technology and analytics are increasingly a part of healthcare and she'd recommend preparing for the future by diversifying your skillset. She cautions people working in the health informatics field not to get pigeon-holed as the person maintaining a legacy system. While it is essential to understand the various systems where data resides today, it is important to take advantage of opportunities to learn new systems and tools where you can.

She would advise people who are looking to apply to a job in this sector to focus on their technical skills, communication skills, healthcare and financial background. List out the programs you've learned or worked with: any specific electronic health records (EHR) systems, analytics tools, word processing (e.g., Microsoft), spreadsheets, remote interface (e.g., Zoom or Microsoft Teams). Ms. Pollack's advice is to include details about projects you worked on and teams you worked with, being sure to tailor it to the role description. Consider your transferable skills. That is, what have you learned or worked on in other roles that might be applicable to the current job opportunity?

There are many opportunities in healthcare payer organizations that train people on the job. It is impossible to know everything about a job because every job is different. Training really depends on the company; sometimes you can get a lot of formal training opportunities and sometimes you might need to help train yourself with documentation and perseverance. Ms. Pollack reminds those interested in advancing in jobs in this area to show that you're curious and willing to learn. She also encourages people to ask for help, as many people enjoy sharing their expertise.

5.5 Day in the Life: HEDIS Analyst

One of the advantages of the HEDIS (Healthcare Effectiveness Data and Information Set) data set is the ability to compare quality across health plans, because the measures are nationally consistent and adopted by over 90% of health insurance providers and many medical providers and practices (Healthy People 2030, 2023). For example, HEDIS measures address a range of health issues, including asthma medication use, controlling high blood pressure, comprehensive diabetes care, antidepressant medication management and advising smokers to quit.

A HEDIS analyst for a major Midwest health insurance payer works on the life cycle of HEDIS. Her project management background is very helpful because the job involves managing her tasks and informing other parts of the organization about what the organization's rates are for HEDIS. Because the company works with providers to try to meet the required metrics, they need to inform providers and talk with them about how they can help to meet these metrics. Using reports, they are able to give updates on these measures. The healthcare payer organization uses value-based care and works with providers to close care gaps, which is the main emphasis of HEDIS. That means if they identify that groups of patients have high blood pressure, they report on gaps in whether those patients were given care to monitor and treat this condition. Once the providers do give care to monitor and treat for this condition, they work to close the "gap" between the diagnosis and care provided. This improves HEDIS scores. If someone has high blood pressure, you want to see that the provider is working with the patient to reduce the blood pressure. There are a few different ways that can be done. HEDIS has specific requirements for what meets that care gap and how that person's blood pressure has gone down to safer levels. That might be medication, but it involves a doctor visit, so when a doctor is prescribing medication, they're using codes and then we use those codes to demonstrate that we're meeting the HEDIS goals.

For HEDIS requirements, the claims data doesn't always give everything they need to demonstrate that the care gap was closed, so analysts have opportunities through supplemental data. For example, certain providers will send blood pressure readings, which means instead of it coming through the claims data, it comes from a secondary source. A few people on the HEDIS team may facilitate that transfer, taking that data, putting it into a usable form and then reporting back to organizations. These are some of the responsibilities of the job.

HEDIS involves a roadmap, like a questionnaire, which requires answering questions about the organization, about membership, medical services, information technology, processing of data and also supplemental data. Documentation is pulled from all these different departments to add to this application. This report then goes to an auditor. The auditor's primary goal is to make sure that the data reported to HEDIS is accurate, so they examine the processes the health plan uses to collect and report data. For example, the auditor may ask questions about the processes used or what might be impacting rate differences from year to year. The HEDIS analyst we spoke to says that she has a background as an English major, writing research papers, so she said it feels like she is writing a massive research paper every year.

5.6 What Kind of Skills Are You Looking for in a New Hire?

The HEDIS analyst responds: "An informatics master's degree is highly sought-after in HEDIS – I think I'm the only one who doesn't have it, but having a coding background helps. We don't code all day, but having the ability to write code or at least know how it is written helps. As far as specific skills, we usually use SQL; database SQL is important. Some of the data analytics like SAS and Tableau would be helpful. Being really organized is important because there is a lot of complexity. A basic knowledge of medical terminology and project management can be helpful. You want to know Excel. I use that every day, all the time."

When asked for her recommendations for those looking for a job like this, the analyst conveys that it is important to include small- and medium-sized companies as well as the larger organizations. The analyst's company is a medium-sized company. She conveys that there are people on her team who came from smaller health plans. She says that meeting deadlines and staying focused are important and it is good to be prepared and eager to learn new skills on the job.

5.7 A Day in the Life: Executive Perspective

Devendra Rao, Executive Director, Information Technology at BlueCross BlueShield Association, discussed how health informaticians work in payer organizations like Blue Cross Blue Shield (BCBS), which has 115 million members in the United States, providing coverage for roughly 1 in 3 Americans.

Mr. Rao states that from a high level, informaticians in a payer organization use information to make members' or patients' healthcare better in terms of both their experience and outcomes. While this is the goal, insurance companies and healthcare providers need to keep costs and premiums low. Cost is an important factor. Payer organizations analyze clinical information to measure the outcomes of various treatments and procedures. For example, informaticians need to look at the clinical outcome from a certain type of procedure and its associated care (e.g., 3 weeks of in-patient rehabilitation vs. 4 weeks of rehabilitation) or whether the outcome differs based on which hospital or specific provider was used. Some analyses look at an episode of care: for example, a certain type of illness, and all the treatment associated with it, across time (e.g., 18 months). To keep track of this, the insurance informatics analysts learn about medical information through claims data using diagnostic codes, billing codes, who the attending physician or care team was, what the facility was and the procedure type. All data about patients or members are de-identified. Insurance organizations may require different analyses and reports for internal stakeholders, investors and clients who may have reports governed by specific rules and regulations.

5.8 Knowledge for Job Hunting

As you consider a job in health insurance or payer organizations, it is important to know that there are both for-profit insurance companies and non-profit government organizations, specifically the Centers for Medicaid and Medicare Services (www.CMS.gov). Each organization needs to fulfill similar tasks in paying for healthcare, documenting their process and demonstrating opportunities for improving quality. However, they may have different approaches to meeting these requirements. One commonality is gathering information to complete regulatory requirements. Overall, these organizations are looking to improve quality outcomes for patients while keeping the costs low. To meet these goals, you likely be involved in learning about a company-wide initiative and helping to fulfill aspects of that plan. Communication with other co-workers and stakeholders in the organization continues to be essential.

There may be additional requirements for CMS employees to meet regulatory requirements for reporting. No matter the organization, there will likely be calendar deadlines to gather information and create reports.

5.9 Job Description Examples

5.9.1 Project Manager

A project manager for a payer organization is responsible for overseeing a project from start to finish. The project manager works closely with other team members to ensure that all deliverables are addressed in a timely manner, with regular communication updates to relevant stakeholders. Project managers may be placed at any part of the health insurance or payer organization, depending on the nature of the project to be completed. Because this role would be taken on in a healthcare organization context, knowledge of healthcare reporting requirements, compliance and information regulations are important.

5.9.2 Business Analyst

A business analyst in health insurance or payer organizations is responsible for collecting, cleaning and analyzing data, then creating reports for business stakeholders. In this capacity, the business analyst works with other business units to understand the specific needs for the analysis and formatting of reports. While some reporting is to meet regulatory requirements, other reporting can focus on process and quality improvement for the payer, its affiliated health providers and clients or patients.

5.9.3 HEDIS Analyst

Other jobs among payer organizations include being an analyst for the Healthcare Effectiveness Data and Information Set (HEDIS), Consumer Assessment of Healthcare Providers and Systems (CAHPS) and Healthcare Outcomes Survey (HOS). Almost 90% of health plans, covering 190 million people, (including HMOs, POS plans and PPOs) use HEDIS to measure performance (www.AHRQ.gov, May 2022). HEDIS is managed by the National Committee for Quality Assurance (NCQA), a private, non-profit organization that accredits and certifies healthcare organizations. A HEDIS analyst may be expected to manage databases, use SQL, write queries to identify trends, draw conclusions, check for accuracy, make recommendations and validate results. Consistent with other jobs in payer organizations, analysts would be expected to collaborate with internal and external stakeholders to address business-related questions and utilize effective verbal and written communication skills to convey information.

5.9.4 Data Strategy and Specialist

This person will work with a product manager to oversee platform data management, collaborating with other key personnel to transfer user requirements into platform functions, planning with third party vendors to develop advanced platform functions to meet the organizations' requirements and focusing on market trends to maintain the competitiveness of products. This position will require experience about product development, product management, data analytics, technical knowledge on common tools for visualization and machine learning. Furthermore, communication skills and teamwork skills are essential.

5.9.5 Information Security Management Leader

Responsibilities include communicating and facilitating between various teams for cyber security, maintaining information security level within the organization to meet certain standards, providing support on information security management systems' maintenance and implementation, performing risk assessment and acting accordingly for different information security issues, improving the user experience of implemented technologies and providing necessary trainings regarding information security. This position requires an education background in computer science with related working experience and relevant certifications in the industry. It is also preferred that the candidate understands concepts and processes of cyber security technologies and risk assessment, is able to make plans for system implementation and management, understand effective project management processes, can work with different teams including global teams and has strong communication and problem solving skills.

5.9.6 Senior Risk Analyst

As a senior position, this position's responsibilities include risk analytics activities, maintaining processes about response escalation and investigation, reviewing daily activities regarding potential violations and risks, leading a team to perform proper risk mitigation activities, and following trends and providing reports addressing risk concerns. This position requires a bachelor's degree in a relevant field, experience of data analytics, information security related certifications, basic coding skills, knowledge of data modeling, specific tools and detection and prevention suites. In addition, leadership, management skills and interpersonal skills are crucial.

5.10 Job Criteria

Criteria of health informatics jobs will vary. Most health informatics-related jobs require at least a bachelor's degree and strong demonstration that you can learn new material. A successful applicant will have familiarity with the processes involved in database management, data analysis, including predictive analytics, reporting, data visualization, security, compliance and policy.

5.10.1 Technical Skills

Familiarity with managing data sets for big data is essential. For a large payer organization like CMS, Kaiser Permanente or BCBS, the analysis of episodes of care are situated in big data sets (e.g., 30–50 terabytes of data). Therefore, the skill sets required to conduct these analyses involve processing, cleaning, managing, storing and analyzing big data sets.

Familiarity with machine learning and artificial intelligence tools for data are growing in importance and frequency of use. Ways to group, clean, normalize data and analyze and report on it will always be required. To that end, robust database tools like Excel are quite helpful, as they are widely accessible and can be used by many people across many organizations.

Awareness of policies and procedures that protect patients' or members' privacy and security is critical. It is paramount for informatics specialists to employ strategies to maintain privacy and confidentiality of the data. You need to be aware of HIPAA and other protections of privacy for patient data. If privacy is not maintained, there is potential for losing patient trust, putting patients at risk, damaging the professional brand and incurring a substantial financial penalty.

Health informatics professionals need to be aware of any organizational procedures to maintain cybersecurity. It is important to be aware that healthcare payer organizations

Recommended Skills

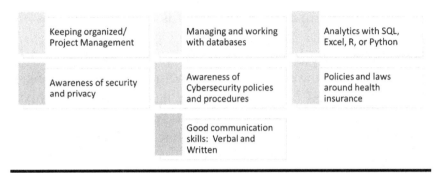

| Keeping organized/ Project Management | Managing and working with databases | Analytics with SQL, Excel, R, or Python |

Figure 5.1   Skills Recommended For Informatics Work in Health Insurance/Payer Groups.

maintain confidential information at vast scale and will have cybersecurity policies to maintain.

Payer organizations and informaticians also need to be aware of state and federal laws regarding health insurance. For example, since the federal Affordable Care Act (2010), it is no longer legal to withhold insurance for those with pre-existing health conditions. Moreover, there are interoperability and privacy/security mandates to be aware of for payer organizations stemming from the federal 21st Century Cures Act (2016).

5.10.2 People Skills

It is important to be a strong collaborator and communicator within and across teams. In particular, it is important to be able to communicate statistical or technical concepts and results to non-technical clients both in written and verbal form. Demonstrating problem solving skills and the ability to think critically is beneficial for the careers in this industry. Dr. Jason Gilder reminds us: "This is not a category to take lightly. Understanding data and trends takes good communication skills."

5.10.3 Experience with Healthcare

Having a clinical background is always going to be helpful in health informatics careers, but it is not required. This is reaffirmed by Dr. Jason Gilder from Optum Labs, noting: "being an RN can provide a lot of background knowledge, but informatics has so much messiness and nuance. I don't think [an] RN is required by any stretch." He has confidence in the process to get a technical person up to speed in working in the health informatics arena, even if they don't have clinical experience.

5.11 International Job Seekers

Many health insurance companies recruit international healthcare professionals. They are usually familiar with hiring those on work visas and H-1B visas specifically for information technology professionals. These employers will look at both technical proficiency and language proficiency in the hiring process.

5.12 Keywords for Job Search

As you search for career opportunities in health information companies, there are some recommended keywords and phrases to start with. Suggestions include:

■ Insurance informatics, database informatics, health insurance data, health information, health insurance informatics, payer informatics, health insurance data policy, HEDIS

5.13 Summary

Many opportunities exist for health informatics specialists in payer/health insurance organizations. It is important to understand their business needs and be ready to bring a database- and analysis-driven skill set in work with data to work independently and with team members to solve health-related business questions. These activities do not happen in a silo, so it is essential to be collaborative with teammates and communicate well with both internal and external stakeholders. As is the case with many organizations using information technology, health informatics jobs may be available as a contractor for both short-term and long-term assignments. There are often opportunities to convert the contract job into a full-time position in the payer organization, so if you do begin working as a contractor, explore options for a permanent role with the group toward the middle to the end of the contract.

References

"Agency for Healthcare Research and Quality (AHRQ)." *AHRQ.* Accessed December 7, 2022. www.ahrq.gov/.

"Accountable Care Organizations (Acos)." *CMS*, December 1, 2021. www.cms.gov/Medicare/Medicare-Fee-for-Service-Payment/ACO.

"Center for Medicare and Medicaid Services (CMS)." *CMS.gov.* Accessed March 29, 2023. https://www.cms.gov/pillar/expand-access.

Compilation of Patient Protection and Affordable Care Act. "As Amended Through November 1, 2010 Including Patient Protection and Affordable Care Act Health-Related Portions of the Health Care and Education Reconciliation Act of 2010 §." 2010.

"Healthcare Effectiveness Data and Information Set (HEDIS)." *Healthy People 2030.* Accessed April 24, 2023. https://health.gov/healthypeople/objectives-and-data/data-sources-and-methods/

data-sources/healthcare-effectiveness-data-and-information-set-hedis#:~:text=The%20Healthcare%20Effectiveness%20Data%20and,report%20quality%20results%20using%20HEDIS.

"Health and Wellness." *UnitedHealthcare*. Accessed December 7, 2022. www.uhc.com/health-and-wellness.

"Home – Centers for Medicare & Medicaid Services." *CMS*. Accessed October 10, 2022. www.cms.gov/.

Raths, David. "Insurers Invest in HealthMap's Kidney Disease Management Approach." *Healthcare Innovation*, May 9, 2022. www.hcinnovationgroup.com/population-health-management/chronic-illness/news/21267001/insurers-invest-in-healthmaps-kidney-disease-management-approach.

U.S. Census Bureau. "Health Insurance Coverage in the United States: 2020." 2020. Accessed June 2022. www.census.gov/library/publications/2021/demo/p60-274.html.

"The Veterans Health Administration." Accessed June 2022. www.va.gov/health/aboutvha.asp.

"Wellness." *The Health of America | Blue Cross Blue Shield*, April 29, 2020. www.bcbs.com/the-health-of-america/topics/wellness#topic-reports.

Chapter 6

Careers in Consulting

"Healthcare consultants need to be able to translate technology into a business domain value proposition."

– Mandi Bishop Meyers
Healthcare Industry Analyst, Gartner

6.1 Introduction to Careers in Consulting

Healthcare generally relies on consultants to provide expertise in areas where they lack in-depth experience. Consultants, rather than being direct employees of the company they perform work for, are hired from an outside consulting company. There are a range of health IT consulting firms. These include boutique, specialty firms, mid-sized and large, national and international firms. Although consulting has been a part of healthcare and the health IT business for decades, there was a significant growth in the number and size of firms as a result of the expansion of electronic medical records.

DOI: 10.4324/9781003185727-6

A few definitions of these types of consulting firms:

▪ Boutique: These are usually small firms which can be run by a single person or a small group. They often specialize in a particular area, such as implementation of a single product, advice on a focused topic, e.g., cybersecurity or connecting customers to other consultants or contractors to address a specific problem.

▪ Specialty firms: These firms focus on a specific area of health IT, such as EHR implementation or optimization, supply chain, laboratory technology or patient engagement. Some may specialize in market sectors, such as government contracting, pharmaceuticals or genomics.

▪ Mid-sized firms: Firms that are more diverse both in their skill sets and areas of concentration.

▪ Large firms: Typically, these firms have the broadest range of skills and areas of specialization. Some may have health IT as one area of the consulting firm. These firms often have offices in several regions of the U.S. and even internationally.

There are also different types of consulting firms. These include: https://payrhealth.com/resources/blog/what-is-healthcare-consulting/

▪ Strategic consulting: This may focus on the "C-level" to define future projects which will benefit the organization with minimal risk. These firms often have research arms which they may publish to the public or for customers only.

▪ Technology consulting: May include assisting an organization in selecting a technology solution, either hardware or software or both.

▪ Legal and regulatory consulting: This includes everything from cybersecurity to HIPAA and other privacy regulations.

▪ Other areas, such as human resources, operations, marketing or revenue consulting.

6.2 Informatics Roles

As you can see, there are many possible roles in informatics consulting. For instance, a senior consultant might assist an organization to select a technology solution. This requires a knowledge of the marketplace of IT products, particularly in healthcare. Depending on the type of firm or the responsibility or specialty area, this might include recommendations on anything from switching EMR products to cybersecurity tools to patient engagement solutions or revenue/coding/billing tools. In each case, the consultant must bring their familiarity with and expertise in these solution sets. It also requires recommendations on the Total Cost of Ownership/implementation (TCO) and potential Return on Investment (ROI).

Another role common in health IT consulting is change management. Changing technology can often be painful and involve resistance to change from some parties in the organization. A senior informatics consultant may be called upon to manage that change. This means understanding the structure and culture of the organization and which stakeholders are pro-change and which are resistant. Identifying executive or physician champions to engage as change makers is key. These champions can help strengthen the case for change by providing their perspective on why the change will have a positive impact. Their status as internal influencers may also be more trusted by some resistant parties than external consultants.

Analysis of industry trends is an important role in strategic consulting. The leadership of healthcare organizations, including the CIO, will seek out advice on what is coming in the next 3-5 years in order to plan investments in technology. A market analysis may develop reports on current directions for specific technologies, such as the Magic Quadrant© or reports on digital health trends or cybersecurity threats. Trend analysis can also be done in person with organizational leadership or by developing custom reports, such as the organization's technology status vis-a-vis health systems that are local or national competitors. Understanding the role of new innovations in health informatics is an important part of advising health systems on new solutions and evaluating the value and risks of adopting these new technologies.

6.3 A Day in the Life

"In consulting, one must distinguish between the tactical and strategic when discussing business and operating models."

– Mandi Bishop Meyers
Senior Consultant, Gartner

It is difficult to characterize a typical day in the life of a consultant. As noted earlier in Roles, this could involve researching, writing or presenting industry trend reports. A day or several days could be onsite at a healthcare facility, gathering information, discussing organizational readiness for new technologies and strategizing with the leadership. This frequently involves travel or virtual meetings with the organization or with widely-distributed teams in the case of larger national consulting firms.

Marcia Conrad-Miller of CGI states that her company does both back-end technology, such as database configuration, and front-end, such as user interface consulting. This can mean utilizing both business analysts and technical positions, such as programmers. She describes three levels they utilize:

■ *Entry-level:* She says, "an entry-level technical person should know how to use technology and implement technology programs; whether it is Python, Java,. NET does not really matter. If you have any experience in health-care, that can help. But it is not required."

■ *Mid-range*: Typically, these will be people who have worked for the healthcare industry and understand how technologies are used in healthcare.

■ *Senior or executive*: Typically, these will be people who are subject matter experts, people who have done ana-lytics, have built models, know what an EHR system is, know what you can expect out of it, do projections and analytics, etc. Senior or executive-level people usually have some clinical background, but it is not required.

She emphasizes the need for people skills as well as project management and the importance of predictive analytics in the future of healthcare consulting.

Mandi Bishop Meyers of Gartner says a day in the life of a consultant might include meetings with healthcare/life science tech leaders or payers on tactical and strategic initiatives in their organizations, such as:

■ Discussing business and operating models
■ Interpreting value in healthcare
■ Competition in retail, big tech
■ Emerging market analysis
■ Talking to tech companies about their strategies and solu-tions spaces

A typical day might include a meeting with health system executives discussing the latest research which will help them develop a strategic plan for digital transformation. A day may involve developing a survey for tech leaders in healthcare on their thoughts about trends or current implementations. Or it could be collaborative teamwork on summarizing trends in the marketplace, such as developing one of Gartner's famous technology hype cycles.

6.3.1 Consultants and Contractors

Some distinguish between the advisor role of consultants and contractors who serve temporary roles in the organization. Contractors are heavily utilized in healthcare IT in a wide variety of roles, often to fill short-term labor shortages or to assist with staffing up for large project implementations. These contractors are typically provided by staffing agencies that specialize in IT or healthcare IT specifically. For instance, installing a new data analytics software or expanding a data warehouse or moving software and data to a cloud provider may require more staff than is available within the organization. Adding these temporary contractors provides the extra hands to complete the project on time and may utilize contractors with specialized skills not readily available within the health system. In some cases, consulting firms can also provide contractors.

6.3.2 Examples of Consulting Firms

The large consulting firms in healthcare and health informatics include some familiar names. These include Deloitte, EY, Gartner and PwC. Many of the large firms work in a variety of industries but have significant healthcare divisions. These firms do research in healthcare trends as well as executive-level consulting with healthcare organizations. Gartner has a specific reputation for information technology consulting and market research and is best known for its Magic Quadrant© reports, which analyze specific technologies, such as business intelligence, cybersecurity and artificial intelligence.

Smaller or boutique firms include companies like Huron Consulting, The Chartis Group and CGI. These are often focused only on healthcare or healthcare IT. These can be rated based on the following factors: (https://mconsultingprep .com/boutique-consulting-firms/)

- Firm culture
- Satisfaction
- Work-life balance
- Level of challenge
- Compensation
- Overall business outlook
- Promotion policies

6.4 Knowledge for Job Hunting

The healthcare consulting business is a dynamic one involving teams in problem solving and advising organizations. Consulting engagements may last for months or even a year or two. Often there are repeat engagements with satisfied customers. Large consulting firms may include consultants in a variety of healthcare areas, not just informatics. For example, a firm may include consultants on everything from strategic planning to finance to human resources. They are also more likely to have market research teams and contracting groups. Boutique firms are more likely to focus in one area, such as healthcare IT, and have smaller teams. Larger firms often expand quickly into new markets, such as digital health and diversity, equality and inclusion (DEI). Because of their awareness of and study of market trends, they are usually responsive to requests for future strategy engagements.

6.5 Job Description Examples

6.5.1 Senior Consultant/Partner

Responsibilities include identifying opportunities with new clients, identify additional opportunities in existing clients, business development including project budget proposals, deliverable development for clients, implementation of process redesign and change management including staffing levels. Additional responsibilities may include direct supervision to assigned employees and allocating work assignments, review of project targets and providing expertise to help organizations improve their business operations.

6.5.2 Quality/Continuous Improvement Consultant

Responsible for assisting client organizations to improve quality and safety and reduce risk exposure. Assist in quality effectiveness through performance improvement processes and regulatory readiness activities. Assess and make recommendations for improvement using quality data and regulatory compliance reports.

6.5.3 Market Analyst

Responsible for analyzing data from various sources to discover insights about the health IT market and identify new opportunities and trends. Combine data sets to discover new insights for clients. Collaborate with other members of the analytics team on advanced analysis of the market, using tools like R or Python. Effectively communicate insights with other internal teams.

6.6 Job Criteria

"Some important competencies for consultants include communication abilities, presentation skills, organizational skills, the ability to work well under pressure, and creativity."
(https://www.mba-healthcare-management.com/faq/ what-is-a-healthcare-consultant/)

Most consulting firms hire experienced professionals, particularly for strategic consulting roles with the C-level. This means hiring those with extensive experience with information within a healthcare organization. A thorough understanding of the structure of healthcare and healthcare regulations is essential. Both in boutique firms and larger firms with specialty departments and special areas of consulting like data analytics, supply chain or laboratory information systems, specialists in those areas, particularly with experience in project management or technology enhancements, are needed. Those with less experience but education in market analysis and trending may qualify for starting positions doing survey work and market trend reports. One recent trend is hiring Diversity or Social Determinants of Health consultants into consulting organizations to meet a formerly neglected area.

Educational requirements can vary as well. For strategic consulting, those with previous experience as a CIO, CMIO or CNIO and a master's or doctorate are preferred. For other areas, a bachelor's degree would be a minimum requirement, with 5 or more years of experience preferred. For leadership positions in consulting, an MBA or similar degree is preferred with a focus on healthcare. There is a Certified Management Consultant designation which can include a healthcare focus (Institute of Management Consultants USA 2022).

6.6.1 Technical Skills

Technical skills in consulting may be less emphasized since understanding the business of healthcare may be more important. However, a basic understanding of what technologies are currently in use is needed. Also, one should have knowledge of innovative technologies which are potential solutions for healthcare organizations. Exceptions to this would be more highly technical areas, such as data center requirements, data analytics capabilities or cybersecurity technologies. More

Recommended Skills

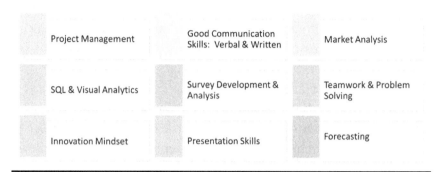

Project Management	Good Communication Skills: Verbal & Written	Market Analysis
SQL & Visual Analytics	Survey Development & Analysis	Teamwork & Problem Solving
Innovation Mindset	Presentation Skills	Forecasting

Figure 6.1   Skills Recommended For Informatics Work in Consulting.

important may be skills in market research, use of spreadsheets and presentation skills.

6.6.2 People Skills

Because consulting requires frequent work with a variety of healthcare workers, people skills are essential. Listening to staff on different levels of an organization and understanding their technology needs and experience level takes patience and knowing how to ask the right questions. In interacting with technologists in the organization, understanding the technology they support, as well as the strengths and weaknesses and stresses they are under, makes for a successful consulting encounter. Interacting with clinical staff, from medical specialists and surgeons to bedside nurses and others, requires listening to their workflow issues, what workarounds they are using due to technology failures and appreciating the day-to-day pressures of hands-on care and patient safety. Finally, the consultant must be able to translate these interviews into recommendations for the current engagement.

6.6.3 Experience in Healthcare

Being a consultant in healthcare requires a thorough knowledge of the industry. Because of the complexity of healthcare and the specific technologies to serve those needs, knowledge of clinical workflow, healthcare regulation and organizational roles is essential to be effective. Also, understanding the unique issues of healthcare economics, workforce requirements, regulations and policy are essential. The few exceptions might be cybersecurity, which is similar to other industries (with the exception of the trend toward ransomware attacks on healthcare organizations) and hardware acquisition. A thorough understanding of the EMR as a core technology in healthcare, the unique challenges of interoperability and the integration of new solutions is a requirement for successful consulting.

6.7 International

Many of the large consulting firms have offices across the globe and often outsource technical tasks to branch offices in other countries. They also offer opportunities within the U.S. for those on work visas. When looking for technical consultants, programmers or analysts, they may turn to international applicants, provided they have the right skill set, people skills and understand the U.S. healthcare environment.

6.8 Keywords for Job Search

As you search for career opportunities in consulting groups, there are some recommended keywords and phrases to use. Suggestions include:

▪ Market research/analysis, market trends, consulting, strategic planning, market surveys, business intelligence, healthcare economic trends, healthcare innovation.

6.9 Summary

Consulting in health informatics provides a wide scope of opportunities. While previous healthcare experience is preferred, there are opportunities to begin by doing market research or other tasks and to be mentored by experienced consultants in the firm. Consulting may involve more travel than many informatics roles, but the benefit is being onsite with a variety of organizations and learning the successes and challenges of each to add to one's knowledge base. There are also opportunities for specialization, whether in a boutique firm or in a specialized department in a larger firm. In some cases, technical skills are less essential than business acumen, especially in strategic consulting. New roles and opportunities are being created in consulting as innovation in health informatics and digital health expands.

References

"Boutique Consulting Firms – Overview & Ranking [2020]." *MConsultingPrep*, February 25, 2020. https://mconsultingprep.com/boutique-consulting-firms/.

"Home." *Institute of Management Consultants USA*. Accessed December 7, 2022. www.imcusa.org/.

"What Is a Healthcare Consultant?" *MBA Healthcare Management*. Accessed December 7, 2022. www.mba-healthcare-management.com/faq/what-is-a-healthcare-consultant/.

"What Is Healthcare Consulting?" *PayrHealth*, June 7, 2021. https://payrhealth.com/resources/blog/what-is-healthcare-consulting/.

Chapter 7

Careers in Senior Care and Long-Term Care

"What is more practical than aging? Practically, everyone will face aging. Whether you are meaning driven, mission driven, money driven, or you have an international focus, focus on seniors, whatever your focus is – this field transforms the capability of information on human well-being in this amazing intersection of information, economy and personal interest."

– Mr. Peter Kress
Senior Vice President and Chief Information Officer of Acts Retirement Life Communities

7.1 Introduction to Senior Care and Long-Term Care

"Senior care" is a broad term and incorporates the many and growing number of health management, prevention and wellness apps, wearables and devices for older adults, generally

DOI: 10.4324/9781003185727-7

interpreted as people aged 65 and older, to improve their own well-being throughout their lives. "Long-term care" is an over-arching term for the field of healthcare that focuses on care of older adults who need some level of ongoing supportive care, rather than acute care. The field includes skilled nursing facili-ties (SNF), long-term post-acute care (LTPAC), assisted living facilities (ALF), short-term rehabilitation and home healthcare agencies (HHA). Both senior care and long-term care rely on health information technology in acquiring, organizing and accessing health data and information to share with clinical teams and patients to help manage the health of seniors.

In terms of health informatics (HI) jobs, there are options such as IT data engineer, systems administrator and director of clinical informaticist. Senior care and long-term care depend on HI positions to build software for employees to use for clinical care or regulatory reporting, utilize telehealth, or to analyze data aggregated to better serve their population.

Adoption of electronic health record (EHR) systems took longer in this sector compared to hospitals and clinician offices, because the long-term care sector was not eligible for federal financial incentives in the HITECH Act (2010) to con-vert paper medical records to electronic health records. This industry was left playing catch-up in terms of upgrading their health IT systems, many of which were self-funded or pri-vately funded. As a result, the informatics and digital health infrastructure has taken longer to establish. Despite being slower to adopt health IT, the industry is an essential compo-nent of health services and continues to expand. This initiative will require health informatics specialists to guide and assist in development of its infrastructure and to optimize opportuni-ties for data analytics.

Long-term care needed to invest in converting to new EHR and digital health tools because their patients are referred from and to acute care hospitals and provider offices that were using electronic health records, health information exchange

(HIE) and direct secure messaging formats. It was imperative to be set up to receive this data in a secure, compliant and efficient way. That is, referrals to long-term care can be done electronically, and if the facilities are not ready to receive those referrals, their business could suffer. Long-term care partners need to have a compliant, secure EHR and a compliant direct secure messaging system to communicate with clinicians at the discharging hospital.

Hospitals' and patients' clinical teams need to ensure that clinical information for the patient is communicated effectively and efficiently for improved quality of care outcomes. Through the Hospital Readmissions Reduction Program (HRRP) and its revisions in 2017 and 2019 (CMS.gov 2023), hospitals could be penalized if the patient was readmitted to the hospital within 30 days of the discharge for certain medical conditions. One of the best ways to ensure that readmission rates stay low is to communicate clinical information for the patient to the medical team in the long-term care or short-term rehabilitation center. To achieve this benefit, hospitals are seeking to refer patients to long-term care centers that have mature digital health programs and can efficiently and effectively receive the digital files. Another benefit of this increased visibility and communication is fewer duplicate tests, resulting in lower costs and less hassle or inconvenience to older adults and caregivers.

Sandy Hebert, Director of Product Analytics at Point Click Care, a market leader in EHR software for LTC and senior care facilities, notes that since the Covid-19 pandemic, greater efforts are being made to improve visibility and communication between hospitals and long-term care facilities. As a result, many more hospitals are now implementing the software (e.g. Point Click Care) from the long-term care facility to improve insight into how best to support patient health outcomes and make any transition of care to and from the hospital to the LTC more informed.

7.2 Health IT to Support Living Independently

Health IT solutions for living independently play an important role in society, especially for older adults who are living independently in the community. In fact, the majority of older adults (93.5%) in the United States live independently in the community, either with family or friends or alone (Wellman & Kinsella, 2010). According to the 2010 Census, 3.1 percent of the older population resided in skilled nursing facilities (West, et al, 2014). The proportion of older adults living in residential care facilities (e.g. assisted living) has been growing. Home health agencies had 4.4 million patients in 2015, with 1.4 million having received services from hospice (CDC 2022). Solutions for facilitating healthy aging in the community are essential and will rely on health informatics specialists to make it more feasible for community-dwelling older adults to communicate their health status, support their needs and to get important medical information and monitoring opportunities to preserve their independence.

7.3 Managing Long-Term Wellness

The field of senior care is transforming to incorporate a spectrum of wellness. There are many digital tools available to consumers for managing their own illnesses and overall wellness. Digital tools available to clinicians and patients need to accommodate receiving information from apps or devices (e.g., personal health record portal, home monitoring systems, Apple watch or Fitbit fitness, continuous glucose monitor, digital images or photos), as well as sending messaging or communication through them. This transformation increases the variety of opportunities for health IT professionals serving this market.

7.4 A Day in the Life: Executive Perspective

To consider health informatics roles in long-term care, we interviewed Dr. Majd Alwan, Chief Strategy and Growth Officer at ThriveWell Tech, focused on transforming senior living. When asked about how health informatics has a role in senior care today, Dr. Alwan described that this sector, as in all of healthcare, is more reliant on data, reporting to regulatory agencies and tracking outcomes. He relays that healthcare in general, as well as senior care, are becoming more reliant upon the EHR and the built-in capabilities like clinical decision support, and new technologies like telehealth.

Dr. Alwan notes that it is critical to have people with a background in health informatics to help in a number of areas of long-term care and senior care, including:

- Planning and implementation of EHR or telehealth
- Customization of systems
- Post-implementation training others on use of platforms
- Taking the use and adoption to the next level/ optimization
- Taking the organization on a journey of using the full capacity/capabilities of the system in the organization

Dr. Alwan describes that analytics teams in long-term care will help to advance capabilities of organizations through three data analytics areas: a) descriptive, b) predictive and c) prescriptive data analytics. Informatics roles in long-term care and senior care have potential for tremendous impact, especially in data analytics. If an informaticist has a strong clinical understanding but is also competent in data, they can become data analysts. Dr. Alwan indicates that by continuing to stack these skills, like financial data with clinical data as well as referral data, it is possible to become the "data guru in the organization," and help not only with clinical decisions, but also business decisions. There is a wide range of applications for data analytics that go beyond descriptive data. This is where the informaticist can use their skills to help the organization to understand the data analysis through predictive modeling, using dashboards or other ways of visualizing data, and even providing decision support.

Dr. Alwan describes long-term care as a great opportunity, because of the tremendous need for insights for quality and efficiency improvement. There is a dearth of these experts for the long-term care sector. Long-term care is positioned to grow, and unlike hospital and payer systems which have already had a leg up and invested in health IT and hired specialists, an informaticist in this space has the potential to be at the top of their field, a "king of the hill," relatively speaking. That is, you could contribute a lot to many aspects of long-term care.

> As a first incentive, I'd think it would also be gratifying because you would know that you are contributing significantly to patient outcomes, and the organization's quality and financial health. This may be unlike when you work for a larger organization, where you start with a smaller role. As a second incentive, it is so gratifying when you are doing something you like or love that is serving a population segment that has been somewhat marginalized, or lacking in delivering quality outcomes. Your work would be helping others.
>
> **– Dr. Majd Alwan**

In terms of the future, Dr. Alwan describes the trend of how much organizations, services, and healthcare use data. The trend, he says, is that we are all producing, consuming, and using more and more data by the day. The amount of data we have to handle and make decisions with (e.g., patient engagement, satisfaction, outcomes, etc.) is growing. Health informatics specialists will be able to bring artificial intelligence (AI) tools to long-term care to help with intuitive visualization, better predictive analytics modeling, decision support and decision making.

7.5 Day in the Life: Long-Term Care Consultant

William Vaughan is a long term care consultant and former Chief Nurse of the Office of Health Care Quality of Maryland. In a recent interview, he notes that one of the benefits of working as an informaticist in senior care or long-term care is that you could be a "big fish in a small pond." Long-term care budgets are stretched, especially after the Covid-19 pandemic. Traditionally, if you said "data in nursing homes" you were likely referring to minimum data set (MDS) data, mandatory reporting for nursing home data to CMS (Medicare and Medicaid). But informatics work in the long-term and the senior care field is changing. For those working in long-term care informatics job roles, there is a lot of opportunity to learn about many facets of informatics work, as opposed to a more limited role. For example, you may be working with new health IT implementations, integrations with other systems, regulatory reporting, analytics or staff training on systems. Moreover, because there are so many integrations with other healthcare partners, like pharmacies, labs and hospitals, it provides an opportunity to learn about the informatics needs of these groups as well. He says:

> Pharmacy in long-term care is more like an IT company. We have 40% of staff involved in integrating nursing homes, preparing software, and reporting

data. For example, some analysis involves figuring out what the cheaper drug is while two drugs have equivalent effects.

These questions can be answered by analyzing data. He notes the tremendous push and pull between the EHR and pharmacies. For example, there are many needs to get orders from the nursing home to the pharmacy safely and accurately. Informaticists will find themselves working on integrations for cases like this, having a tremendous impact on quality care. These examples of pharmacy or lab integrations are some of many tasks you may be working with on a daily basis, including a new implementation of an electronic health record, clinical decision support or telehealth system.

Informaticists also need to talk with facility staff about their workflow and how they currently do their job of capturing health data, what areas of that workflow they like and what needs to be improved. Informaticists also work with long-term care staff to troubleshoot how to run certain regulatory reports or analyze data about readmission rates to hospitals. Informaticists in long-term care need to communicate with informatics teams at hospitals and health IT vendors to make sure all stakeholders have what they need. Through these interactions, you'll likely be learning both technical and procedural information about how to optimize these systems, enabling these information tools to help facility staff to deliver the highest-quality care and be aware of issues they need to address.

7.6 Informatics Roles

Job roles are emerging in all sectors of senior care, including home health agencies, health IT innovation/startup companies, assisted living, mobile x-ray, mobile health services, home monitoring, rehabilitation centers and long-term care. Health informatics job roles are essential to improve health, well-being and quality of life for seniors as they live independently in the community and in residential care communities or long-term care settings.

The emphasis of using health IT in nursing homes traditionally has been more around reimbursement, not health outcomes (Salmond and Echevarria 2017). As a result, there have not been as many clinical informatics roles in long-term care compared to other job sectors. However, this is changing. More long-term care facilities are leveraging health IT by utilizing electronic health records (EHRs), Health Information Exchanges (HIE) and telehealth systems. These all improve quality of life for patients. Use of health IT systems can help to cut costs as analytics from pharmacy, lab and other expenses can lead to more efficient selections.

7.6.1 Clinical Informatics

Clinical informatics entails someone who can assess, plan, implement and evaluate hardware and software applications integrated with the electronic health record. Informatics functions can include application support, business architecture management, enterprise data management, content management, system optimization, change management, requirements management and partnership management. Someone in these roles should also be familiar with clinical information systems (e.g., an electronic health record or CPOE), accreditation and regulatory standards and program development. This kind of role is aligned with the many facilities that utilize sophisticated health IT systems.

7.6.2 Small Teams or Solo Practitioner

Not all of the long-term care industry has advanced its use of health IT, and there are many other facilities with challenged infrastructure, workflow and practice that have a long way to go. In those places, Wi-Fi can seem "advanced" in some buildings. Individuals wear multiple hats, where you might have one IT person helping a number of internal stakeholders. Or, a director of nursing or member of the nursing staff may be the unofficial informatics specialist as they help to assemble appropriate reports for regulatory agencies. Some long-term care organizations might have one IT person or a more robust resource through a full department. Other, larger organizations are more likely to have an informatics team or specialists to provide consultation across a number of long-term care facilities.

7.6.3 Sharing Information

There is a growing need in senior and long-term care settings to capture and share clinical information electronically. Because of this need, it is important for informatics roles in this sector to integrate with critical data systems, identify the relevant fields of data and content and manage that content based on requirements for the organization. This includes regulatory bodies for quality reporting, as well as medical or clinical teams to inform clinical decision support. Many long-term care facilities work with local hospital electronic health record systems (Meehan 2017) through liaisons who are employed at area hospitals but offer care on site at the long-term care facility. Most SNF and ALF are moving toward clinical information systems, electronic referral systems and data sharing in health information exchanges (HIE), but it is likely more advanced in larger organizations than smaller. Data sharing capabilities and reporting are a primary focus for senior and long-term care because patients with complex medical histories are moving in for various lengths of time, and often have follow-up appointments with specialists or other clinicians, or are seen in an emergency department. These transitions of care, both to and from other sites and clinical settings, require data sharing, updates of health status, medications and treatment plans. Health informatics roles support this exchange and utilization of data to inform patient care. Informatics roles also include application support of the various EHRs and other integration points with outside systems.

7.6.4 Roles in Home Monitoring Systems and Wellness

Senior care is more than nursing homes and long-term care; it also encompasses mobile and wearable technology to promote wellness among seniors. Informatics roles are emerging in home monitoring systems and consumer health IT, enabling seniors, or anyone with health challenges, to live independently in their own home in the community. These informatics roles are found in the health IT innovation space for wearable health monitoring devices (e.g., glucose monitors, heart rate monitors) and the related software to upload pertinent data and provide analytics and meaningful alerts to caregivers and clinicians should the senior need assistance. Informaticians are also needed in developing software and devices, analyzing data and creating reports for other home monitoring systems (e.g., motion sensor systems in the home to note if someone has fallen) and wellness apps.

7.6.5 Roles in the Financial and Regulatory Context

The demand for senior care continues to grow, yet financial margins in nursing homes have been thin for many years. Ever since the Covid-19 pandemic, there has been a disproportionately heavy financial impact on the industry of long-term care due to decreased census and occupancy levels. William Vaughan noted: "Before the pandemic, if a facility operated at 90–95% occupancy, they had a decent opportunity to get by financially. In the post-pandemic world, U.S.-based long-term

care facilities are often operating below this occupancy thresh-
old, making it a challenge."

Facilities want to provide the best care for patients,
and reimbursement is an essential component of this.
Reimbursement, in turn, is tied to reported quality ratings. In
long-term care, reported ratings include (but are not limited
to) the Minimum Data Set (MDS) – used to measure quality of
care – and Medicare Advantage (see www.Medicare.gov) – a
newer category of Medicare that permits some reimbursement
for long-term care. The need to meet these data capture and
reporting responsibilities will continue to increase opportunities for clinical and other informaticists in this area.

7.6.6 Integration with Pharmacy and Other Health Specialists

Long-term care and senior care facilities have informatics job
roles involved with integrating pharmacy and other health
specialist information with health information systems (e.g.,
EHRs) in terms of administration and reporting. For example,
if patients get treatment and care from nutritionists, physical
therapy, occupational or speech therapy, documentation of
this care may be in separate peripheral systems that need to
connect to the primary EHR. Informaticists who can be aware
of the requirements of end-users to see up-to-date information for patients' prescriptions, therapy regimens, insurance
reports, etc. have necessary roles.

The Covid-19 experience has also emphasized the importance of the integration of long-term care health information
systems with both pharmacy and laboratory systems. While
this need has always existed, during the Covid-19 pandemic
when seniors needed to be isolated with limited exposure
to others, the need to keep important information accessible
was paramount. As a result, many long-term care facilities
improved the integration points to get results and pharmacy
prescriptions faster. This results in job opportunities for

informaticists who are helping to bridge the gap between these stakeholders.

7.7 Knowledge for Job Hunting: Demographics

Opportunities to serve the senior care and long-term care sectors will continue to grow based on market demand and demographics. Globally, the number of persons aged 65 years or over in 2020 was 727 million (United Nations 2020). This number is projected to more than double, reaching over 1.5 billion in 2050. The United Nations (2020) reports that the proportion of the population aged 65 years or over is expected to increase from 9.3% in 2020 to around 16.0% in 2050. These numbers are consistent with population projections in the United States. According to the U.S. Census Bureau (accessed July 29, 2021), there were more than 54 million U.S. residents 65 years and older on July 1, 2019. This number is projected to grow to 94.7 million adults over the age of 65 by the year 2060. Adding to this trend is the estimate that between 2015 and 2050, the population of those aged 85+ is projected to more than triple in the United States (AARP 2018).

7.8 Job Description Examples

7.8.1 Director of Clinical Informatics

Responsibilities include leading a team to develop and improve protocols and procedures on medical records related technical workflows and enhance the usage of clinical data, collaborating with IT professionals to utilize applications and making decisions as needed. As a senior role, extended years of experience in healthcare settings and electronic medical records are required, while long-term care experience can be a plus. Strong leadership, problem solving skills, organizational skills and communication skills are necessary. Specific licenses may be needed depending on employers' requirements.

7.8.2 IT Data Engineer

This person will need to help the whole cycle of development and implementation of new applications and maintain existing applications, ensure the performance of applications and servers within the organization, work with technical standards as needed, solve technical problems and issues and conduct technical projects as needed. Experience or degrees in computer science or related areas and programming language knowledge are necessary. This position also requires strong leadership, communication skills and management skills.

7.8.3 Systems Administrator

This person will provide support for the organization's systems, including every step of the systems life cycle. This person is also expected to implement new technical tools to the existing environment to better organize data and provide necessary services. Suggestions on potential directions of additional technical projects, performing regular system and database maintenance and developing system utilization guidelines are needed. This position requires a degree and experience in information technology, informatics or related areas, abilities to identify and solve system issues, teamwork skills, decision making skills and communication skills.

7.9 Job Criteria

7.9.1 Technical Skills

For those who work in long-term care and senior facilities, it is important to understand what information is necessary, who needs to see it and how they need to use it. Informaticists might be working with team members from finance or administration, regulatory, patient care or hospitals and health IT business partners. Informaticists will likely need to discuss and learn about the problem to be solved or initiative to support. Part of this discovery process involves talking with the relevant stakeholders to identify which data fields are required and why, how to display them on a report, who needs it and by when or how often. Informaticists evaluate existing workflows and work with staff members to create necessary modifications that make sense for the team. It is helpful to understand or be ready to learn information systems and have the ability to run data analysis based on specific requirements for regulatory, quality measures, special programs, or from clinical practitioners or administrators. Moreover, technical training skills are also needed to help other colleagues within the organization to be able to design and use information systems correctly. For those who work in technical roles related to long-term care or long-term care affiliates, it is helpful to be familiar with building reports, integrative standards (e.g., FHIR, RESTful API, HL7, etc.), programming languages (R, Python), database management (data dictionaries, SQL) and analytical skills (Advanced Excel, SAS).

Recommended Skills

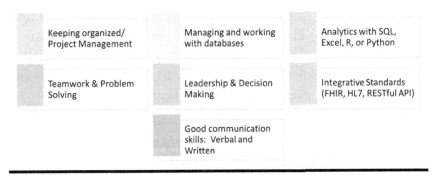

Keeping organized/ Project Management	Managing and working with databases	Analytics with SQL, Excel, R, or Python
Teamwork & Problem Solving	Leadership & Decision Making	Integrative Standards (FHIR, HL7, RESTful API)
	Good communication skills: Verbal and Written	

Figure 7.1 Skills Recommended For Informatics Work in Long-Term Care/Senior Care.

7.9.2 People Skills

Remember, a good attitude and willingness to learn will take you far in life. In long-term care and senior facilities, informatics staff need "people skills" or soft skills in order to collaborate with clinical practitioners, administrators, patients, family members and stakeholders, both from inside the senior care setting and outside as other stakeholders send and request information. It is important for a person working with the informatics team to be able to think analytically and problem solve. These tasks require talking to people, including co-workers and related stakeholders. For example, senior care facilities may need to upload and receive information for compliance or clinical partners in hospitals, pharmacies, physical therapy, radiology, etc. In order to capture and report the correct data to inform decision making, it is helpful for informaticians to have strong communication skills, both verbally and written, as well as relationship building skills. The informatician needs to interact with staff and stakeholders at all levels in order to optimize workflows and understand how to mitigate issues that arise. Skills in change management and project management are helpful in achieving these goals. In software development/health IT companies, IT staff need to participate in projects which involve several team members or communicate with customers to help solve problems or collect feedback. Communication skills are crucial for working in this field. Since IT staff and clinical practitioners may have different vocabularies based on their expertise, it is helpful for health informatics workers who work as a liaison between these groups to have familiarity with both healthcare and technical terms and processes.

7.9.3 Experience with Healthcare

There are job opportunities in informatics in long-term care and senior facilities that require healthcare experience, and those that do not. For example, clinical informaticist roles generally require being licensed as a nurse or having other healthcare experience in order to expedite communication among clinicians using health information systems. Other data analyst and informaticist roles do not require healthcare clinical experience, but instead look for strength in information science, analysis and communication. Many senior care and long-term care informatics centers hire non-clinicians as part of their organizational team.

7.10 International

Long term care or senior care organizations may recruit international healthcare professionals through work visas and H-1B visas specifically for information technology professionals. These employers will look at both technical proficiency and language proficiency in the hiring process.

7.11 Keywords for Job Search

As you search for career opportunities in senior care and long-term care organizations, there are some recommended keywords and phrases to try. Suggestions include:

- Long-term care informatics, data analytics, senior care informatics, aging services informatics, senior care health IT, quality of care for older adults, life course informatics, information science

7.12 Summary

Long-term care and the senior care industry offer a growing opportunity for health informatics professionals based on the need for people who are familiar with health and information systems and have the ability to identify and communicate needs to a variety of stakeholders. Those working in long-term care and senior care settings will need to leverage both technical and people skills to work with digital tools and information required for care and regulatory requirements for quality when caring for older adults in either institutional or home settings. Based on demographic trends, this industry sector will continue to grow, with innovation geared toward information technologies that support independent and socially connected living in the community.

References

Centers for Disease Control and Prevention. *CDC*, 2022. https://www.cdc.gov/nchs/fastats/home-health-care.htm.

Committee on Energy and Commerce. "Implementation of the Health Information Technology for Economic and Clinical Health (HITECH) Act: Hearing Before the Subcommittee on Health of the Committee on Energy and Commerce, House of Representatives, One Hundred Eleventh Congress, Second Session, July 27, 2010 §."

"Hospital Readmissions Reduction Program." *CMS.gov*. Accessed April 24, 2023. https://www.cms.gov/Medicare/Quality-Initiatives-Patient-Assessment-Instruments/Value-Based-Programs/HRRP/Hospital-Readmission-Reduction-Program#:~:text=Section%201886(q)%20of%20the,Year%20%5BFY%5D%202013.

Houser, Ari, Wendy Fox-Grage, and Kathleen Ujvari. "Across the States 2018: Profiles of Long-Term Services and Supports – AARP." *AARP*, 2018. www.aarp.org/content/dam/aarp/ppi/2018/08/across-the-states-profiles-of-long-term-services-and-supports-full-report.pdf.

"H-1B Specialty Occupations, DOD Cooperative Research and Development Project Workers, and Fashion Models." *USCIS*, July 21, 2022. www.uscis.gov/working-in-the-united-states/h-1b-specialty-occupations.

Meehan, Rebecca. "Continued Access to Hospital Patient Health Record Data in Long Term Care: User Experience Study." *Journal of Applied Gerontology* (August 2017): 1–20. https://doi.org/10.1177/0733464817723565.

Salmond, Susan W., and Mercedes Echevarria. "Healthcare Transformation and Changing Roles for Nursing." *Orthopaedic Nursing* 36, no. 1 (2017): 12–25. https://doi.org/10.1097/nor.0000000000000308.

United Nations Department of Economic and Social Affairs, Population Division. "World Population Ageing 2020 Highlights: Living Arrangements of Older Persons" (ST/ESA/SER.A/451), 2020. https://www.un.org/development/desa/pd/sites/www.un.org.development.desa.pd/files/files/documents/2020/Sep/un_pop_2020_pf_ageing_10_key_messages.pdf.

US Census Bureau. "Older Population and Aging." *Census.gov*, September 20, 2022. www.census.gov/topics/population/older-aging.html#:~:text=According%20to%20the%20U.S.%20Census,million%20on%20July%201%2C%202019.

"Welcome to Medicare." *Medicare*. Accessed December 12, 2022. www.Medicare.gov/.

West, Loraine, Samantha Cole, Daniel Goodkind, and Wan He. "65+ in the United States: 2010, Current Population Report"; 2014. U.S. Department of Health and Human Services, National Institutes of Health, National Institute on Aging, U.S. Census Bureau.

Wellman, Nancy and Kinsella, Kevin. "Size and Demographics of Aging Populations." In *Providing Healthy and Safe Foods as We Age: Workshop Summary*. Washington, DC: National Academies Press, 2010. https://www.ncbi.nlm.nih.gov/books/NBK51841/.

Chapter 8

Careers in Government

"Working in government roles requires patience with the bureaucracy but gives one the opportunity to influence national policy and to interact with a broad constituency of those wanting to have a say in policy."

– Lygeia Ricciardi
Founder, AdaRose, previously Director of Consumer Health for ONC

8.1 Introduction to Careers in Government

Opportunities in government agencies are plentiful. The role of the federal government grew particularly during the American Recovery and Reinvestment Act of 2009, which spawned the Meaningful Use program through the Office of the National Coordinator for Health IT (ONC). This program incentivized health systems and hospitals to install electronic medical records (EMRs) with the condition of using them in meaningful ways governed by a series of regulations. The ONC still exists today, and although its role has shifted away

DOI: 10.4324/9781003185727-8

from Meaningful Use, its focus remains on promoting the use of health IT to improve care. This includes standards development, interoperability and infrastructure. (www.healthit.gov/topic/about-onc)

Other federal agencies with significant health informatics roles include the Department of Health and Human Services (HHS), of which ONC is a part. Specifically, HHS includes the Center for Medicare and Medicaid Services (CMS). This large agency oversees billions of insurance claims and regulates healthcare payment for these programs. Since there is a vast amount of healthcare data, a significant health informatics staff is required to maintain these services. These jobs also serve some of the agencies within HHS, such as the Indian Health Service, the Food and Drug Administration (FDA), the Centers for Disease Control and Prevention (CDC) and the National Institutes of Health (NIH). (www.hhs.gov/careers/job-search)

One of the largest employers for health IT in the federal government is the Veterans Health Administration (VA). Its reach comprises 1,243 healthcare facilities, including 170 VA Medical Centers and 1,063 outpatient sites of care. The VA had its own EMR built in-house but is now transitioning to the EMR from a major vendor. The Office of Electronic Health Record Modernization (OEHRM) manages deployment of the new system. (www.ehrm.va.gov/)

As a massive and national health system, the VA has many health informatics roles, some centralized and many others at local facilities. Similar to large health systems, these roles include maintaining and supporting the EMR, infrastructure, cybersecurity, patient-facing portal and apps, interoperability, etc. (www.va.gov/health)

In addition to federal roles, state and local governments have health informatics jobs that can be equally fulfilling. Many of these are in public health informatics as part of managing data for health departments. The Covid-19 pandemic has demonstrated on the importance of accurate data on public health to address these types of challenges. Another state-level health IT service is the Health Information Exchange (HIE). These are typically initiated by states, although some have outsourced to contractors. However, HIEs have struggled to sustain a viable business model, and some have shut down. State Medicaid offices also require strong participation by health IT professionals to process claims and generate reports. New public health initiatives to improve health and wellness as well as those addressing environment and health will require strong informatics support.

In many cases, especially at the federal level, health IT services are contracted out to private companies. There are many companies that work primarily on government contracts. This work encompasses everything from creating reports on quality initiatives, such as those from the Agency for Healthcare Research and Quality (AHRQ), to creating and maintaining databases of public health data. Government agencies frequently issue RFPs (Request for Proposals), which are funding opportunities for contractors. Much like grants, they are competitive and may be short- or long-term projects.

8.2 Informatics Roles

Those informatics roles which support direct patient care, such as the Veterans Health Administration or Indian Health Service, are similar to those at other hospitals and health systems, including everything from customer support to EMR implementation and support to leadership roles such as CMIO, CNIO and CIO. In federal agencies, there are many opportunities for system analysts as well as a focus on policy analysts. Policy analysts help write policies based on legislation, such as the 21st Century Cures Act (2016) which "is designed to help accelerate medical product development and bring new innovations and advances to patients who need them faster and more efficiently" (FDA 2020). Policies and regulations go through review cycles (typically 90 days), which are called comment periods, based on the initial version of the policies and proposed regulations. A policy analyst would review these comments (often hundreds but could be thousands) with the team and propose changes in the form of final rules.

There are also IT specialists and technical information specialists who work for agencies within HHS, such as the FDA, CDC, NIH or CMS. These roles may work with policies as well as with disease surveillance, drug evaluation or adverse events or clinical trial management. For the Food and Drug Administration, jobs may include creating and managing large databases, such as for adverse drug events or approved digital health products. Jobs at the Centers for Disease Control and state health departments may also involve management of public health databases for specific infectious diseases (such as Covid-19) or databases related to vaccine administration with detail down to the county or city level. For the National Institutes of Health, the focus would be on research informatics and grants, including the management of research studies at the various institutes that make up the NIH and databases and applications related to grants from the application process through the posting of results. At the Centers for Medicaid and Medicare and state agencies that manage claims through these programs, there are a variety of roles. A major portion manages claims made to these programs as well as programs which detect fraud. Within CMS, there is the CMS Innovation Center, which establishes and evaluates new programs to improve effectiveness and efficiency in healthcare.

8.3 A Day in the Life

A typical day depends on the specific role and agency in government. One thing is certain: you will be dealing with

policies and regulations. Whether your role is specifically
to develop regulations based on legislation and policy or
you implement a new program or software, regulations will
determine how you perform these tasks. Understanding and
interpreting standards is particularly important if you are
dealing with interoperability, for instance. If your full-time
job is policy and regulation, such as in the ONC or FDA, you
will be writing proposed regulations, reviewing stakeholder
comments on the proposed regulations and finalizing the
regulations. For instance, the 21st Century Cures Act required
regulations on Information Blocking (www.healthit.gov/topic/
information-blocking). Many comments were received and
reviewed before the final rules were issued in 2022. If the job
is installing or maintaining software or devices or managing
security or infrastructure, it may be more similar to IT roles in
hospitals or other industries. Many government agencies are
utilizing innovative solutions, either created within an agency
or from startups. Consultants and contractors will also spend
time reviewing and writing Requests for Proposals (RFP) or
Requests for Information (RFI) and watching legislation which
may bring new opportunities.

> "One of the most rewarding aspects of working in
> government is the national scope of policy develop-
> ment and interacting with people from around the
> country who want to influence health informatics
> policies."
>
> **– Lygeia Ricciardi**
> *Founder, AdaRose, Previously Director of
> the Office of Consumer e-Health, ONC*

Lygeia Ricciardi worked for the Office of the National
Coordinator for several years and found the experience
rewarding for both developing national standards and receiving comments on proposed standards from all over the

country. She knew the limitations of government work and the need to work through large bureaucracies with complex policies and procedures. Realizing the importance of good people skills both in group meetings and on a one-to-one level is key. Also, understanding the government agencies to collaborate with and their scope and 3-letter acronyms (CDC, FDA, etc.) is necessary for success in these positions. As with many jobs in IT, approaching deadlines can be stressful; in Lygeia's case, this was the release date for both draft policies and the incorporation of comments into final policy statements.

8.4 Consultants and Contractors

As mentioned earlier, a significant number of health IT services in government are outsourced to consulting firms or contractors. These can be short-term projects, such as reports or program evaluations, or longer-term implementations of new software (for instance, the new EMR for the VA). These projects can be complex based on the legislation and regulations related to the tasks, and usually require a Request for Proposal (RFP) or bidding process up front. Most firms that work on government contracts have experts and templates to help smooth this process. These RFPs can have long timelines with strict deadlines. Once a project is funded, the funding period can be for months or even years, with the opportunity to extend the deadline in some cases. Strong project management to meet deadlines and stay within budget are key to success with these projects.

8.5 Knowledge for Job Hunting

Upon applying for a federal government job for the first time, it is important to understand the different job levels and salary ranges. Also, because of the size of the bureaucracy and the complexity of federal regulations, the hiring process can be longer than private industry and requires some patience and persistence.

On the state and local level, the job titles and descriptions may vary widely. It could be a data manager or analyst for a state HIE (health information exchange) or for a county health department. Or on the infrastructure side, one could manage a data center for a state Medicaid program or the email and messaging system for a city board of health.

8.6 Job Description Examples

8.6.1 Public Health Analyst (ONC)

"Serving as an expert analyst in developing, monitoring, implementing, and evaluating current or projected complex, interrelated public health programs involving governmental and non-governmental organizations from multiple sectors at the community, state, and national levels. Coordinating activities and negotiating agreements that have far-reaching impact. Serving as lead representative, project officer, or comparable position for administration of a comprehensive, cooperative agreements. Providing technical advice and assistance in monitoring, managing, and evaluating cooperative agreements, grants, and/or awards. Researching and preparing responses to ad-hoc or recurring inquiries received in writing or telephonically (e.g., Congressional briefing materials and responses). Collecting and compiling qualitative and quantitative information and data for use in program decisions." www.healthit.gov/topic/careers-onc

8.6.2 Health IT Policy Analyst

Analyze public policies related to topics including interoperability, patient engagement, HIPAA, clinical decision support and artificial intelligence. Prepare new policies for comment periods. Review and analyze policy comments to summarize and present recommendations for changes before final policies are issued. Respond to policy questions from providers and organizations. Present at national meetings as requested.

8.6.3 IT Specialist/System Analysis (CDC)

"The purpose of the position is to perform a wide variety of duties related to the design and development of database systems; the development of programming specifications for those database systems; and the review and reporting of information technology (IT) security and/or system development life cycle (SDLC) standards." www.usajobs.gov/job/684812300

8.7 Job Criteria

Job criteria in government agencies is dependent on the job roles. Previous experience with policy and regulation is a plus. Policy analysis skills are needed for higher-level positions, especially federal. Many policy analysts have master's or doctorates related to healthcare or an MBA with relevant healthcare experience. Jobs maintaining or installing software would be similar to those jobs in other industries while following specific regulations required by the agency. That includes working with approved vendors and contractors. As with most general IT positions, a bachelor's degree in computer science or a related field is required.

8.7.1 Technical Skills

Technical skill requirements vary by the type of government position. Policy analysts must have an understanding of the industry they are regulating. That means knowing how EMRs

Recommended Skills

Project Management	Policy Analysis
Good communication skills: Verbal and Written	Teamwork & Problem Solving
Innovation Mindset	Integrative Standards (FHIR, HL7)

Figure 8.1   Skills Recommended For Informatics Work in Government Roles.

work, IT security, and some understanding of networks and data centers. Also, a working knowledge of quality measures is needed since that is often included in regulation. For those supporting software or infrastructure, skills similar to those in other industries are needed, although the specific software may have been specifically designed for a government agency and the security requirements may be unique. Government contractors must have technical skills appropriate for the work they are contracted for. This could include an understanding of health IT systems to develop reports or skills specific to a software install. For any government position, ongoing training is essential, especially as policies and regulations change and affect IT systems.

8.7.2 *People Skills*

People skills are essential for those working in government. The range of stakeholders one needs to collaborate with is broad and can include health systems, payers, providers, contractors, professional associations and even lobbyists.

In addition, government work is done in teams or teams of teams. Interagency work is common and collaboration with legislators and their staff is key to moving ahead with new policies and funding.

8.7.3 Experience in Healthcare

Typically, experience in healthcare is preferred for government healthcare work. The exception may be those supporting specific software or infrastructure. Because of the complexity of healthcare policy and regulation, those doing analysis in this area must have at least some experience in healthcare or policy. Some on-the-job learning can occur, but it is challenging to get up to speed with the various areas of policy: from standards to reimbursement to security, to mention a few. Because of the centrality of the EMR in healthcare today, it is essential for anyone seeking a position in government health IT to have some knowledge of the products and clinical workflow within them.

8.8 International Job Seekers

Federal government jobs require U.S. citizenship for job applicants in most cases. There is an exception – if the agency finds it difficult to recruit a citizen for a specific position, they may choose to recruit someone with a green card or other special status (Library of Congress 2023).

8.9 Keywords for Job Search

As you search for career opportunities in senior care and long-term care organizations, there are some recommended keywords and phrases to try. Suggestions include:

■ Program evaluator, system analyst, public health analyst, consumer health, interoperability, privacy analyst, cybersecurity specialist, IT specialist, project manager. See, for example, Careers at ONC: www.healthit.gov/topic/careers-onc and HHS www.hhs.gov/careers/job-search

8.10 Summary

There are a range of careers in government for health informaticists. These careers fall primarily into two categories:

1. Policy analysis
2. Technical support and implementation

Policy analysis can occur in federal, state and local levels and requires a knowledge of both the legislative and regulatory processes and also the software and technical tools one is regulating. Policy analysts can be within government or in professional societies, consultant groups or payers and vendors. Those in government supporting, implementing or upgrading software or systems need solid technical skills with an understanding of government regulations. Because of the broad range of stakeholders for government agencies and the complex teams and interagency work, good people skills are essential for any of these positions.

References

"About ONC." *HealthIT.gov*, September 8, 2022. www.healthit.gov/topic/about-onc.
"Careers at ONC." *HealthIT.gov*, December 8, 2022. www.healthit.gov/topic/careers-onc.

"Citizenship Requirements for Federal Employment: Immigration Law and Federal Employment." *Library of Congress.* Accessed March 24, 2023. https://www.loc.gov/careers/working-at-the-library/frequently-asked-questions/citizenship-requirements-for-federal-employment/.

"FDA." *Fda.gov*, 2020. https://www.fda.gov/regulatory-information/selected-amendments-fdc-act/21st-century-cures-act.

"Information Blocking." *Information Blocking | HealthIT.gov*, October 31, 2022. www.healthit.gov/topic/information-blocking.

"It Specialist (Systems Analysis)." *USAJOBS.* Accessed December 12, 2022. www.usajobs.gov/job/684812300.

"Job Search." *HHS Careers.* Accessed December 12, 2022. www.hhs.gov/careers/job-search.

"Pathways to Public Service: Minority Serving Institutions Project." Accessed December 12, 2022. www.healthit.gov/sites/default/files/page/2022-02/MSI_Project_Overview.pdf.

"Transforming Health Care for Veterans, Revolutionizing Health Care for All." *VA EHR Modernization*, Accessed December 6, 2023. https://digital.va.gov/ehr-modernization/?redirect=ehrm.

"VA for Vets: Your Gateway to VA Careers." Accessed December 12, 2022. www.vaforvets.va.gov/.

"Veteran's Health Administration." *Va.gov.* Accessed December 6, 2023. www.va.gov/health.

Chapter 9

What Professional Associations Are Saying

What Kinds of Work Do Health Informaticists do?

In this chapter, we will discuss:

1. What professional associations (HIMSS and AMIA) are saying about health informatics competencies in the profession
2. International opportunities
3. Perspectives on where we are going in health informatics in the 21st century

9.1 Health Informatics Professional Competencies

Professional associations in the field of health informatics, including the Healthcare Information and Management Systems

Society (HIMSS) and The American Medical Informatics Association (AMIA), are working to identify, evaluate and communicate professional standards and best practices of the field of health informatics. AMIA continues to advance efforts in informatics workforce development. For example, an AMIA taskforce (2016) developed recommendations addressing workforce development needs at the chief clinical information officer level within healthcare organizations. The AMIA First Look Program addresses workforce disparities among women, including those from marginalized communities (Bright, et al 2017). Moreover, AMIA leads projects in delineation of practice of health informatics roles (Gadd, et al, 2020). HIMSS conducts an annual workforce survey to ascertain how the profession is developing, and is involved through its TIGER initiative (Technology Informatics Guiding Education Reform) in international health informatics competencies. HIMSS continues to conduct research in workforce development through its Leadership and Workforce Survey (https://www.himss.org/resources/himss-leadership-and-workforce-survey-report) and the Nursing Informatics Workforce Survey (www.himss.org/resources/insights-2022-himss-nursing-informatics-workforce-survey-exploring-current-state-and). Accessed May 30, 2023. These continued efforts provide the industry with ongoing research identifying trends and gaining valuable insights into the rapidly changing market for healthcare and IT professionals (www.himss.org, 2023).

9.2 HIMSS (Healthcare Information and Management Systems Society)

When we consider the type of work health informaticists are doing or will do, it is important to inform the people working in these roles by identifying core competencies that will prepare them for participating in the field. The HIMSS group, Technology Informatics Guiding Education Reform (TIGER), provides the global health workforce with innovative informatics/eHealth tools and resources to transform health (HIMSS 2023). The global network of TIGER collaborates to integrate informatics/eHealth into healthcare education, certification, practice and research through an inclusive, interdisciplinary and intergenerational approach (HIMSS 2023). In order to measure, inform, educate and advance eHealth and health information technology skills, work and workforce development throughout Europe, the United States and globally, the TIGER International Initiative conducted the EU*US eHealth Work Project (http://ehealthwork.org/, 2020). One of the related projects in the initiative will help healthcare professionals globally to better meet the requirements of an interprofessional process and outcome-oriented ways of providing modern care (Shaw et al. 2020). It is the first international effort to identify core informatics competencies for nurses in various roles, inclusive of inter-professional coordination of care and quality management.

Hübner and colleagues (2019) describe the methodology and developments towards the TIGER International Recommendation Framework of Core Competencies in Health Informatics 2.0. This framework is meant to augment the scope from nursing towards a series of 6 other professional roles, i.e., direct patient care, health information management, executives, chief information officers, engineers and health IT specialists and researchers and educators. Health informatics core competency areas were compiled from various sources that had integrated the literature and were grouped into consistent clusters. These core competency areas were evaluated by 718 professional experts from 51 countries. Among the top 10 competency areas across various job types, ethics in health IT, communication and leadership were consistently ranked as important (Hübner et al. 2019). Depending on the job role you have, you may be required to analyze data, manage information or implement IT while understanding the care process and maintaining quality and patient safety. See their report for information about a variety of job roles in the health informatics field (Hübner et al. 2019).

Overall, this HIMSS/EU*US eHealth Work Project initiative helps to elucidate the types of proficiencies relevant to common job roles and health informatics education to improve quality and patient safety through health information technology.

9.3 AMIA (American Medical Informatics Association)

AMIA assembled a practice analysis task force of health informatics practitioners from a variety of informatics practice areas, who drafted a preliminary list of practice domains and associated tasks, knowledge and skills. They next conducted an online survey of health informatics professionals, AMIA members and members of clinical healthcare associations. Based on results of the survey, Gadd and colleagues (2020) published a position paper for AMIA to describe what health informatics professionals do and what they need to know in order to do it.

The AMIA paper outlines a delineation of practice (DoP) for work in health informatics. Their study represents the first time HI professionals have been surveyed to validate a description of their practice. Their method included an online survey distributed to 1011 HI professionals to validate a delineation of practice for health informatics, developed by six independent subject matter experts drawn from a group of health informatics professionals, representative of various practice areas of HI. Respondents included "health

informatics professionals" or practitioners with clinical informatics (e.g., dentistry, nursing, pharmacy), public health
and HI or computer science training. They worked across
different types of organizations and work settings, including healthcare providers, public health agencies, universities, industry and consulting firms. While respondents spent
most time as practitioners (45% of their time), many others
were educators, consultants or researchers. Many disciplines
were represented, including nursing (26%), health informatics
(21%), medicine (not limited to MDs, at 12%), public health
(12%), pharmacy (7%) and dentistry (3%). The results of
the practice analysis included five domains of HI work (see
Figure 9.1), along with 74 related tasks, and 144 knowledge
and skills.

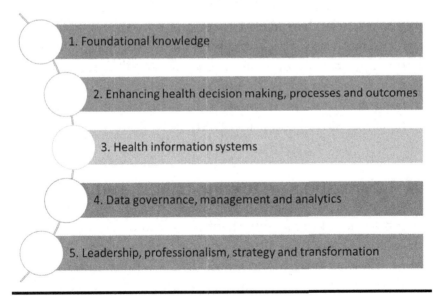

**Figure 9.1   The Five Domains of HI Practice Determined from the
AMIA Report.**

Source: Gadd et al. (2020), **used with permission.**

The practice areas outlined by AMIA include 1) foundational knowledge, 2) enhancing health decision making, processes and outcomes, 3) health information systems, 4) data governance, management and analysis, and 5) leadership, professionalism, strategy and transformation (see Figure 9.1). Taken together, these areas offer a preview of the types of work you will likely participate in, and the knowledge and skills you will need to support the work.

9.3.1 The Takeaway

Careers and everyday jobs in health informatics continue to evolve and will require people who can communicate and demonstrate leadership. Jobs in this field will continue to emerge as digital health technologies, including artificial intelligence (AI) tools, become more embedded into healthcare. For those who can understand the broader issues, what the problem is, how their skills can help to solve the problem and how to complete a project independently or collaboratively, there will be many opportunities. Professional organizations need the engagement of practitioners and people working in the field to help them accomplish their initiatives and advance the field. Consider getting involved.

9.4 Information on Joining HIMSS and AMIA

The professional organizations of HIMSS and AMIA are important leaders in health informatics professions offering online informational webinars for discussion around timely health informatics topics. Current health informatics-related job listings are available on their websites and through their jobs pages: https://jobmine.himss.org/ and https://jobs.amia. org/jobs/. Both organizations offer educational programs, information on innovation and advancements in the field, professional development and updates on regulatory changes. It may be beneficial to become a member of either or both organizations. This information can be found at their respective websites: www.HIMSS.org and www.AMIA.org. For those who are students, there may be discounts applied to membership.

9.5 Training and Education

Most careers in health informatics require the applicant to have at minimum a bachelor's degree. The degree does not necessarily need to be healthcare-focused. As mentioned in previous chapters, an applicant's demonstration of their solid work ethic and a willingness to learn can take them far. For many jobs, an advanced certificate or master's degree in a health informatics-related area is preferred. There are several master's degree programs in health informatics and biomedical informatics. These programs can be offered in person, hybrid or online, depending on the university.

Kent State University, the academic home of the authors, offers both a 100% online post-baccalaureate certificate (18 credits) and a 100% online Master of Science degree in health informatics (36 credits). The Kent State health informatics programs have been in place since 2011, with a strong track record of student success. Courses are offered in an asynchronous 7-week format, so that students can take 2 classes per semester, one at a time (first 7 weeks, followed by second 7 weeks). As a result, students can complete the certificate in one year or less, and the master's degree in 2 years or less. The online format tends to accommodate students who are working full-time and need the flexibility of the online, asynchronous format. The website is here: www.kent.edu/ischool/health-informatics. Please feel free to contact the authors of this book for more information.

Online education can vary, so it is important to look for programs that have a history of offering up-to-date and relevant content in formats that accommodate your schedule and have a focus on quality and excellence in delivery of information in an online environment. Other resources to identify graduate certificates and programs can be found through the HIMSS Approved Education Partners website as well as AMIA's informatics academic programs site.

As mentioned in earlier chapters, job seekers may find it beneficial to explore professional certifications. The Certified Associate in Healthcare Information and Management Systems (CAHIMS) and the Certified Professional in Healthcare Information and Management Systems (CPHIMS) are both available. It is recommended that a preparation course is taken before taking the test. The AMIA Health Informatics Certification (AHIC) is available to take, and may be most attainable for those who have been working in the field or are in a master's program and who have been instructed in the foundational domains of the field. These certifications help employers to know that you are interested and willing to learn more about the health informatics field. For many, these types of certifications help refresh their knowledge. Job seekers should not expect these to get them the job; however, having certifications like these can strengthen the applicant's case for being engaged and interested in learning more in the field.

9.6 International Medical Graduates and Global Professionals

Careers in health informatics can be advantageous and rewarding as alternative career paths, especially for those who are international medical graduates (IMGs) (Turin et al. 2021).

IMGs are graduates from medical schools located outside of the country where the medical graduates intend to integrate professionally (Turin et al. 2021). As the IMG transitions to gaining medical licensure in a new country, they are well positioned to apply their knowledge in health informatics, and may benefit from master's programs or bridging programs in health informatics as alternative career pathways for international medical graduates (Turin et al. 2021). Global professionals in fields related to health informatics may find a pathway to any number of stakeholders looking for specific talent for their organizations.

9.7 Job Postings in Health Informatics

When you look across common job postings that have "health informatics" in the description, you start to see some of the common elements and background employers. One study by McLane and colleagues (2021) conducted a cross-sectional study examining 206 health informatics job posts to understand industry needs for health informatics-related knowledge, skills and competencies. Their results showed that bachelor's degrees in related fields were the most frequently required education in the job posts evaluated, along with practical experience in the field. Health informatics job posts in the study overall required EHR support, training and knowledge of other clinical systems skills. A clinical background, which commonly required RN licensure and clinical experience, was advantageous for professionals in health informatics positions, but not required in all postings. The authors (McLane et al. 2021) recommended that industry and academia alike should adhere to shared definitions of commonly used terms to ensure understanding and the mutual benefit of preparing graduates to meet industry needs. While health informatics terms are being defined and used more consistently, job postings for health informatics still have a great degree of flexibility in how the job role is defined relative to the title.

9.8 Knowledge Areas of Clinical Informatics

Ongoing analysis on work roles in more specific health informatics areas, like clinical informatics, continues to inform us about what types of experience and information are helpful to work in this area. Aligned with AMIA's five domains of HI practice (Gadd et al. 2020), Brouat and colleagues (2022) examined unique knowledge and experience areas among healthcare professionals working in clinical informatics. Their analysis, based on a systematic literature review, resulted in the identification of nine knowledge and experience domains. These included:

1) health sciences and services,
2) professionalism and clinical practice skills in healthcare,
3) information science and technology,
4) health informatics specialization,
5) communication,
6) financial planning and management,
7) analytical assessment and decision making,
8) education and training,
9) leadership and change management.

Brouat and colleagues (2022) call for the need to develop professional competency standards for job roles in clinical informatics in the further development of the field. Further work needs to be done to delineate competency standards for job roles in all areas of health informatics, including consumer health informatics and public health informatics.

9.9 Health Informatics in the 21st Century

No matter the sub-specialty, health informatics should be a required skill for 21st century clinicians (Fridsma 2018). The development of information technology has brought significant changes in the healthcare industry, leading to a new foundation of health information as digital health. However, the effective utilization of data is still a problem for many clinicians and healthcare stakeholders. In order to bridge the gap between health practitioners and health IT companies to better understand information and increase benefits to patients, health informatics training is essential, with special attention to digital health literacy in informatics. Fridsma (2018) outlines that both the U.S. and England have implemented programs to help increase awareness of the importance of health informatics education and provide guidance on useful resources. It is crucial to keep focusing on providing essential health informatics training for all stakeholders across business domains, including those highlighted in this book: healthcare, long-term care, government/research, consulting, health IT companies and payers/insurance companies. Healthcare professionals require this training in order to understand data and its role in improving healthcare services.

Hersh and colleagues (2014) describe competencies related to health informatics to be achieved in medical education, writing: "Physicians in the 21st century will increasingly interact in diverse ways with information systems, requiring competence in many aspects of clinical informatics." The specific competencies the paper addresses include:

- Information retrieval
- Effective use of the EMR
- Use of clinical decision support
- Protect privacy and security
- Use data to promote patient safety

- Engage in quality measurement
- Use health information exchange
- Appropriate use of telemedicine/virtual care
- Participate in practice-based research

9.10 Summary

Thought leaders and practitioners, as well as professional associations, like HIMSS and AMIA are working to monitor global progress in health informatics job roles. The delineation of practice reports help stakeholders in the field, including job seekers, educators and employers to more clearly identify roles and tasks to be performed to maintain and improve quality of care as informed and facilitated by digital health. With this clarity comes an opportunity to align education and training programs to support either those people who are currently in the job, or those seeking the job. It is important to seek out continued education opportunities to be aware of changes in the field.

References

AMIA Task Force on CCIO Knowledge, Education, and Skillset Requirements (2016) (led by Joseph Kannry); https://www.hcinnovationgroup.com/clinical-it/article/13026510/amia-outlines-workforce-development-guidelines-for-chief-clinical-informatics-positions

"AMIA Home, Front Page: American Medical Informatics Association." *AMIA*. Accessed January 17, 2023. https://amia.org/.

Brouat, Sophie, Clare Tolley, David Bates, James Jenson, and Sarah Slight. "What unique knowledge and experiences do healthcare professionals have working in clinical informatics?" *Informatics in Medicine Unlocked*. Vol. 32 (2022). https://doi.org/10.1016/j.imu.2022.101014.

Bright TJ, Williams KS, Rajamani S, Tiase VL, Senathirajah Y, Hebert C, McCoy AB. Making the case for workforce diversity in biomedical informatics to help achieve equity-centered care: a look at the AMIA First Look Program. J Am Med Inform Assoc. 2021 Dec 28;29(1):171–175. doi: 10.1093/jamia/ocab246. PMID: 34963144; PMCID: PMC8714276.

Fridsma, Douglas B. "Data Sciences and Informatics: What's in a Name?" *Journal of the American Medical Informatics Association* 25, no. 1 (2018): 109. https://doi.org/10.1093/jamia/ocx142.

Gadd, Cynthia S., Elaine B. Steen, Carla M. Caro, Sandra Greenberg, Jeffrey J. Williamson, and Douglas B. Fridsma. "Domains, Tasks, and Knowledge for Health Informatics Practice: Results of a Practice Analysis." *Journal of the American Medical Informatics Association* 27, no. 6 (2020): 845–52. https://doi.org/10.1093/jamia/ocaa018.

"Health Informatics." Kent State University. Accessed January 17, 2023. www.kent.edu/ischool/health-informatics.

"Healthcare Information and Management Systems Society." *HIMSS*, January 13, 2023. www.himss.org/.

HIMSS U.S. Leadership and Workforce Survey; https://www.himss.org/resources/himss-leadership-and-workforce-survey-report; accessed May 30, 2023.

HIMSS Nursing Informatics Workforce Survey; https://www.himss.org/resources/insights-2022-himss-nursing-informatics-workforce-survey-exploring-current-state-and; accessed May 30, 2023.

Hersh, William R., Paul Gorman, Frances Biagioli, Vishnu Mohan, Jeffrey Gold, and George Mejicano. "Beyond Information Retrieval and Electronic Health Record Use: Competencies in Clinical Informatics for Medical Education." *Advances in Medical Education and Practice* (2014): 205. https://doi.org/10.2147/amep.s63903.

HIMSS. 2023. https://www.himss.org/what-we-do-initiatives/technology-informatics-guiding-education-reform-tiger.

Hübner U., J. Thye, T. Shaw, B. Elias, N. Egbert, K. Saranto, B. Babitsch, P. Procter, and M. J. Ball. "Towards the TIGER International Framework for Recommendations of Core Competencies in Health Informatics 2.0: Extending the Scope and the Roles." *Studies in Health Technology and Informatics* 264 (2019): 1218–22. https://doi.org/10.3233/SHTI190420. PMID: 31438119.

"Jobs, Work & Careers – Healthcare It Opportunities." Accessed January 17, 2023. https://jobmine.himss.org/.

McLane, Patrick, Cheryl Barnabe, Brian R. Holroyd, Amy Colquhoun, Lea Bill, Kayla M. Fitzpatrick, Katherine Rittenbach, Chyloe Healy, Bonnie Healy, and Rhonda J. Rosychuk. "First Nations Emergency Care in Alberta: Descriptive Results of a Retrospective Cohort Study." *BMC Health Services Research* 21, no. 1 (2021). https://doi.org/10.1186/s12913-021-06415-2.

"Medical Informatics Jobs – American Medical Informatics Association." Accessed January 17, 2023. https://jobs.amia.org/jobs/.

Shaw, Toria, Rachelle Blake, Ursula Hübner, Christel Anderson, Victoria Wangia Anderson, and Beth Elias. "The Evolution of TIGER Competencies and Informatics Resources Executive Supplemental Report (HIMSS)." 2020. https://www.himss.org/sites/hde/files/media/file/2020/03/10/the-evolution-of-tiger-competencies-and-informatics-resources-final-10.2017.pdf.

Turin, Tanvir C., Nashit Chowdhury, Mark Ekpekurede, Deidre Lake, Mohammad Lasker, Mary O'Brien, and Suzanne Goopy. "Alternative Career Pathways for International Medical Graduates towards Job Market Integration: A Literature Review." *International Journal of Medical Education* 12 (2021): 45–63. https://doi.org/10.5116/ijme.606a.e83d.

Chapter 10

Career Phases and Next Steps

Like careers in many professions, there are multiple stages progressed through over time. This chapter will be divided into four phases of career development:

- Starting out
- Early career progress
- Mid-career development
- Senior career/leadership development

Not all career progression is this linear, but we will use this as a template for the typical experience in health informatics.

10.1 Starting Out

Careers in health IT can have different starting points. Some begin directly out of high school, perhaps starting out at a help desk at a health system while going to college. Others may begin with bachelor's degrees in information technology

DOI: 10.4324/9781003185727-10

or nursing or related fields. Some in medical fields who have the clinical background and understanding of healthcare software and technology may enter as clinical analyst or support of the Electronic Health Record (EHRs). So health informatics teams may include those with strong backgrounds in technology even from industries outside of healthcare, while others have strong clinical backgrounds with an understanding of workflows and medical terminology. Successful teams mix these skills to provide the best technical and clinical outcomes. As mentioned previously, internships are another on-ramp to a career in healthcare informatics. Most of these are part of academic programs, but some may be found through organizations like HIMSS and AMIA.

10.2 Early Career Progress

Those with a few years of experience in health informatics begin to have a broader understanding of the breadth of the field through projects and work with their own teams and other teams in technology implementations and support. Many in the field seek continuing education to enhance their skills, whether through an educational institution, through the health system or through a software company, such as a company that sells and supports an EHR. In addition, early careerists often pursue certification. Certifications may be in a specific area (i.e., cybersecurity) or related to a specific software, and can be obtained from a college or university, a vendor or a professional health IT organization, such as HIMSS (Healthcare Information and Management Systems Society) or AMIA (American Medical Informatics Association). Certifications in specific specialty areas or modules of EMRs are typically available through the hospital system utilizing the software.

Another characteristic of early careers in health IT is gaining a deeper knowledge and specialization on the specific software, technology, workflows and usability in their area of expertise. Some may look to change areas, while others gain more depth in their chosen area. Some may seek broader opportunities, such as project management, which gives one opportunity to work in a variety of informatics areas. Working in a project management office in a health system, for instance, means working on implementation of EMR modules, a new Customer Relationship Management (CRM) system, new supply chain software or supplying computers and networking to a new building. Many health systems look for specialization, particularly around the EMR vendor product, so that vendor certifications can increase your value as an employee going forward.

Networking with others in health informatics is key to career development at this stage. Fortunately, there are many opportunities for networking in health IT. For example, HIMSS has chapters in most US states, which have one or more conferences per year as well as golf outings, speaker series or other networking events. Software companies frequently provide user conferences, which offer networking opportunities with others who are supporting that software throughout the country. National meetings also provide excellent networking opportunities, including those sponsored by HIMSS and AMIA. Also, newer national and regional meetings promote health technology innovation. Networking with fellow professionals provides not only learning from others, but also understanding of other career paths as well as job opportunities in other companies and health systems.

Online networking is another effective tool for career development. The broadest tool is LinkedIn.com. This website/app allows one to create a professional profile similar to a resume, including job history and membership in organizations. Then one can connect with or follow others in the profession to develop a broader network. LinkedIn also posts job opportunities customized to your interests, and job recruiters utilize it to find qualified candidates. Other online networking sites include those from HIMSS and AMIA through committees and special-interest groups.

Mentoring provides an essential path for learning the profession and gaining advice on career advancement. Early in one's career is the right time to seek out an experienced mentor in the field, meet regularly and discuss career goals, skill development and new opportunities. There are three types of mentoring:

1. Traditional One-on-One Mentoring
2. Distance Mentoring
3. Group Mentoring (https://hr.ucdavis.edu/departments/ learning-dev/toolkits/mentoring/types)

Pick the type that fits you best. Decide whether to seek a mentor within your company or outside. Find influencers in your area of interest on social media or through local or national organizations.

Consider the "4 Key Facets of Successful Mentoring Relationships":

■ Consider compatibility. The most successful pairings are based on an honest assessment of requisite strengths and weaknesses of both mentor and mentee
■ Prioritize quality over quantity
■ Match supply with demand
■ Communicate candidly (www.inc.com/entrepreneurs-organization/4-key-facets-of-successful-mentoring-relation-ships.html)

Mentoring, networking, certifications and skill development will help lead you to the next stage of your career.

10.3 Mid-Career Development

At this phase in your career, you can put your full skill set to use. Demonstrating your knowledge of health informatics in specific projects will lead to more opportunities with increased responsibilities. Many at this stage take on project management or team leadership roles. Project management may come naturally to some based on earlier involvement in implementation projects in a healthcare organization. For instance, as a project team member implementing a new EMR module or new cybersecurity tool, one is acquainted with the multiple steps involved in a complex project and the importance of cross-team collaboration. At the same time, successful project management requires specific training and, in many cases, certification as a project manager. (www.pmi.org/certifications/ project-management-pmp) Some organizations encourage Six Sigma training, particularly in the area of quality or process improvement. (www.sixsigmacouncil.org/) Also, as healthcare organizations utilize advanced analytics with teams of data scientists, understanding their role as a team member is essential. Knowing how data scientists work and what problems to refer to them for deeper analysis is key to their success.

Similarly, with team leadership or supervisory responsibilities, one may have experience with good or poor leadership styles and know some of the methods that are more effective in motivating and leading teams. However, those with a technical background may have deep technical skills but lack strengths in managing people. People skills are often lacking in IT managers. This is where specific training in supervision and management is essential. There may be training opportunities within your organization, such as Servant Leadership. (www.shrm.org/resourcesandtools/hr-topics/organizational-and-employee-development/pages/the-art-of-servant-leadership.aspx). People skills in health informatics are also needed to work with customers, internal or external, to understand their needs and find technical solutions which improve workflows and work satisfaction.

In the process of taking greater responsibility mid-career, it is important to consider leadership training in preparation for the next step. There is always the challenge of fewer opportunities at the top of a career pyramid, but with new digital health companies and more innovation within healthcare organizations, the next career steps are broadening.

10.4 Senior Career/Leadership Development

At the highest level of leadership, often the CIO or CMIO, the responsibilities are significant and time constraints are constant. One CIO noted that his day was filled with 30-minute meetings from at least 8am to 6pm. Informatics leadership roles continue to expand. For instance, many healthcare organizations now have Chief Nursing Information Officers, Chief Information Security Officers, Chief Research Informatics Officers, Chief Data Officer and others for digital health/ transformation and innovation. In addition, startup companies provide similar opportunities for even the role of CEO for those with informatics backgrounds and Chief Medical Officer for physician leadership.

There are important networking groups for this level. The best known is CHIME (College of Healthcare Information Management Executives). There are also special opportunities within organizations, such as becoming a HIMSS Fellow or an AMIA Fellow (https://amia.org/communities/famia/ fellows-amia).

Health informatics leaders participate in the leadership group of healthcare organizations and need to not only manage the information technology department, but also lead initiatives and budgets for major projects which will improve care and operations of the organization overall. A strong relationship with the CEO is essential. CIOs and other IT leaders work with strategic consultants to plan for the future, as well as work with industry solutions to manage and initiate new technologies for the organization.

10.5 Next Steps

As mentioned earlier, career progression may not be linear. In the current health IT industry, it is not uncommon for professionals to move across industry segments in the course of their work life. For instance, Lygeia Ricciardi began her career with a research firm, then worked for the federal government in the Office of the National Coordinator for Health IT, then did health IT consulting around patient engagement, worked for a startup and now has begun her own startup. Others have moved from health system IT departments to consulting firms or industry companies, including software vendors. With the growth of innovative start-ups around the country, there are many career opportunities with new healthcare technologies and services. Additionally, the field of Diversity, Equity and Inclusion has created new opportunities in consulting firms and technology companies.

10.6 Remote Work

Since the epidemic, remote work or work from home has become routine. While some IT workers have returned to work in the office at least part-time, the use of remote desktop support, virtual private networks (VPNs) and cloud computing have made many IT tasks feasible as 100% remote. Video conferencing enables most meetings to be virtual and has developed new roles in IT to support this technology both for meetings but also for virtual care of patients. Some healthcare organizations are now hiring informatics employees as 100% remote both to limit the office space needed and also to broaden the recruitment process. There are pros and cons to remote work – making space in your home for private work, having a reliable wireless internet connection and having contact with co-workers by phone and video conferencing only. Having to come into an office usually means regular hours and a commute but also face-to-face interaction with co-workers and other teams.

Remote work has significant implications for those with disabilities. While hospitals and health systems have appropriate accommodations for those in wheelchairs or other disabilities, other health informatics employers may not. However, in most cases where remote work is allowed or even preferred, everyone, including people with disabilities can take advantage of these opportunities, which have become more common since the Covid pandemic. While employers cannot ask about health conditions during job interviews, discussion of reasonable accommodations, required by law, should be discussed after the hiring process has been completed. Most job descriptions will be clear about physical demands of the job so that, for instance, if lifting of equipment is required, that should be stated up front. However, many technical positions do not require lifting or other physical demands.

10.7 Conclusion

Throughout this book, you can see the breadth of the field of health informatics and its growth both in the number of jobs and in the variety and changing landscape. Hopefully, this book will serve as a catalyst for identifying and pursuing your next career move in the health informatics field. Health informaticists solve problems in health and healthcare using data and information. Creative solutions and strategies in health informatics will continue to grow in importance as our society continues to leverage more data for decision making. No matter the domain (hospitals, health insurance, health IT, consulting, government or long-term care) in which you decide to work, you should be able to build upon your versatile skill set as you move forward in your career. We encourage you to make a difference and to start this exploration process today!

References

"College of Healthcare Information Management Executives." *CHIME*, December 8, 2022. https://chimecentral.org/.

"Fellows of AMIA." *AMIA*. Accessed December 12, 2022. https://amia.org/communities/famia/fellows-amia.

"HIMSS Member Advancement." *HIMSS*, October 11, 2022. www.himss.org/membership-participation-member-advancement.

"Official Industry Standard." *The Council for Six Sigma Certification*. Accessed December 12, 2022. www.sixsigmacouncil.org/.

Pattani, Ajay. "4 Key Facets of Successful Mentoring Relationships: Guiding Others Toward Growth Can Be Mutually Rewarding. We Share Some Best Practices." *Inc.com*, 2017. www.inc.com/entrepreneurs-organization/4-key-facets-of-successful-mentoring-relationships.html.

"PMP Certification | PMI – Project Management Institute." Accessed December 12, 2022. www.pmi.org/certifications/project-management-pmp.

Tarallo, Mark. "The Art of Servant Leadership." *SHRM*, May 17, 2018. www.shrm.org/resourcesandtools/hr-topics/organizational-and-employee-development/pages/the-art-of-servant-leadership.aspx.

"Types of Mentoring." *Human Resources*, October 28, 2022. https://hr.ucdavis.edu/departments/learning/toolkits/mentoring/types.

Index

C

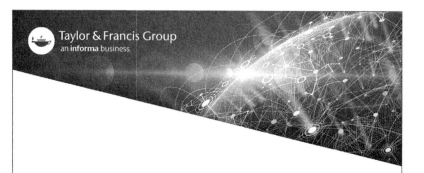

Printed in the United States
by Baker & Taylor Publisher Services